The Auto-Sell.

The Key to Creating Star Performers
and to Becoming a Star Yourself

By Award Winning Author

Dr. Barry Borgerson

Second place in a national contest

for best business book for 2011.

Reader Views Literary Award

2-Selfs Publishing Company
5805 Clovis Ridge Dr
Wake Forest, NC 27587

ISBN: 978-0-9838150-1-3

For more information, contact Barry Borgerson at Barry@2Selfs.com or visit the book's website at http://www.Auto-Self.com.

Preface

*If you manage people, what could <u>they accomplish</u> if you knew how to **guide them** to leverage their talents and transform their counterproductive habits?*

*What would <u>you attempt</u> if you knew someone could **guide you** to transform to achieve it?*

This book opens up the next frontier in recognizing, understanding, and improving those ubiquitous activities that humans do independent of their intentions and outside of their normal awareness.

Struggling To Succeed Consistently At a High Level

Jerry led the quality assurance department of an engine manufacturing company. His career advancement stalled because he could not motivate people outside of his organization to produce needed results and he could not develop his team members to operate at a higher level. Jerry was a highly skilled individual contributor but he could not lead effectively, and he could not understand why his company would not promote him. Jerry was blind to the fact that he lacked fundamental leadership tools to motivate others, to change the underperforming habits of some of his team members, and to hold people accountable.

Alan was a rising star consultant in a firm that catered to CEOs in Fortune 100 companies. Then, his career and his personal life started to go downhill. In spite of repeated attempts, he could not control his anger. His frustration and his jeopardy mounted as he struggled to understand why he could control so many aspects of his life but seemingly had no way to manage his dysfunctional behaviors.

Jerry and Alan, whom we will discuss later, are typical cases of people who do not have the insights and techniques to motivate and develop others or to gain control over their own undesired behaviors. If you examine your own automatic behaviors and actions or if you ask people close to you to reveal them to you, you will discover that some enhance your success and some do not serve you well. This book reveals the root causes of Jerry and Alan's deficiencies and those of many others. Perhaps you will recognize some of yours. You will also acquire techniques to leverage your talents and overcome your deficiencies in your professional and personal life and to enable others to do the same.

Maximizing the Effectiveness of Others

The success of all leaders who have others reporting to them, from first-line supervisors to CEOs, depends on taking decisive actions to maximize the performance of their direct reports. You may have told people you lead that you want them to improve their effectiveness. Sometimes that may achieve the results you desire and other times not. Do you know why they often do not and indeed cannot improve on their own? This book enables you to determine when your team members need *greater knowledge* and when they need *different behaviors* to improve their performance. It provides techniques for you to **guide** them to overcome their barriers to attaining greater results from their latent talents and to transform their undesirable habits.

Beyond Self-Help

Have you tried on your own and failed to change an unwanted habit that interferes with your success at work or in life? If so, you need this book, which you can use to empower somebody to act as a **transformation guide** to enable you to change an unwanted behavior. You will learn why this method is *inherently* more reliable than self-help efforts. You can also use the techniques in this book to **guide** a friend or colleague through transformational behavior change.

This book bridges the gap between inexpensive but frequently insufficient self-help approaches to changing counterproductive behaviors and the level of investment required to retain a professional behavior-change coach.

The Second Mode of Human Activities

These breakthrough opportunities for guiding others to improve their performance, or for getting someone else to coach you to achieve at a higher level, accrue from a fundamental insight explained in this book: humans operate in two different modes – a *thinking* mode and an *automatic* mode. The automatic mode controls more areas of human activities and affects our success more broadly than most educators, organizational leaders, and trainers previously realized.

This revelation of a dual mind creates an "ah ha" experience for nearly everyone when they encounter it, and normally causes them to recall some missed opportunities of their own and recognize counterproductive habits of many people around them.

This book identifies our two distinct modes as causing us to, in effect, have two different "selfs" – a **thinking-self** and an **auto-self** – that vie for control of our actions and thoughts. *The Auto-Self* also leverages this two-selfs insight to create a theory of the inner workings of both modes. The advent of this emancipating **two-selfs theory** enables us to visualize human activities through a new conceptual "lens" and to construct and use reliable techniques for managing the auto-self to create positive change in many aspects of life. This allows us to establish a new way of doing, leading, and being for ourselves and to empower others to do the same.

Conquering our auto-self, our automatic mode of behaviors and thought patterns, is the *next frontier* in maximizing achievement, overcoming undesired behaviors, and sustaining success on a broad spectrum of issues and in many disciplines, professions, and other aspects of life.

The underlying nature of the auto-self is not complex, but it is different from the normal way of thinking about the mind and maximizing performance. To make the auto-self more accessible, this book uses many visual illustrations and six types of distinctive callout boxes to create a solid understanding of the inner workings of our two selfs.

Explanatory Callout Boxes

Types of highlight boxes	Explanations
Definitions	Because this book introduces new material, it provides explicit definitions.
Principles	This box type identifies the underlying principles that govern our automatic mode of activities. Summarized in Appendix A
Properties	To understand the inner-workings of our two "selfs," we have identified several corresponding properties of both modes. This book develops 8 properties involved in habit change. Summarized in Appendix B
Techniques	Identifies specific techniques that readers can use to guide others through transformational habit change. Summarized in Appendix C
Insights	Useful insights into the inner-workings of our two selfs but not at the level of a fundamental principle.
Sidebar	Material related to our two selfs but not directly involved in transforming undesired habits.

This book stands alone. It contains sufficient content to empower you to transform undesirable behaviors. This is also the first in a series of books on the foundational *two-selfs* principle, on the nature of the automatic mode of human activities, and on how to improve various aspects of our auto-self to achieve one's goals in life and to establish sustainable competitive advantages for organizations.

As you will learn, our automatic mode affects our success at work and in life in several crucial ways. This first book focuses on changing habitual behaviors and describing the two-selfs theory and systematic techniques for transforming counterproductive habits.

Acknowledgements

I offer my deepest gratitude to the following people who read and provided helpful enhancements and editorial feedback on this book.

My son, Eric, has patiently edited multiple versions of my work on this topic over several years. Eric's keen philosophical interest launched in his undergraduate days and his attention to detail from his legal writing enabled him to suggest better ways to describe my concepts and identify some points that enhanced this book.

Anthony Policastro, a multi-published author, provided a great service by working his way through a more technical manuscript to simplify my writing and create better narrative.

John Ermanni, a vice president at Compuware Corporation and an executive my organization previously coached, has read multiple versions over the years and contributed very helpful feedback.

Craig Mathews, CEO of Big Think, Inc. whom I currently have the pleasure of coaching, worked his way systematically through the manuscript and provided many helpful suggestions for improvements.

Michael J. Burns, Executive Vice President of the American Society of Employers, reviewed the manuscript and offered useful suggestions for improvement. My company has worked with Mike over several years to provide coaching services through ASE.

Tom Torma, the head of administration and people development for Cadillac Products Automotive Company and an executive I have coached and trained as a coach, read my latest manuscript and offered many constructive insights.

Dan Nelson, who created the clever illustrations in this book, ignored what I asked him to draw but listened carefully to the points I wanted to illustrate. He then used his artistic creativity to draw illustrations that are different from what I had imagined. (Facebook/DanTheArtMan; DanNelsonArt.com)

Finally, I want to thank my wife, Carol, who patiently (usually) endured my extensive research and writings on the work reported here and my family, friends, colleagues, and clients who contributed in many ways over the years to the concepts and insights in this book. Too many other people contributed to acknowledge them by name, but I offer my sincere appreciation to all of you.

Barry Borgerson
Raleigh, NC
September 21, 2011

About the Author

Dr. Barry Borgerson, Founder and President of Complete Leadership, Inc., is a pioneer in understanding and managing the internal mechanisms that control automatic behaviors, hidden thought patterns, and other so called "soft" success factors. The unique combination of his executive leadership experience, deep understanding of the automatic mode of human activities, and the development and use of systematic habit-change techniques has enabled him to help leaders reliably transform to execute at previously unachievable levels.

Barry graduated from the University of California, Berkeley with a Ph.D. in Computer Science and a minor in Human Resource Management.

Barry led the design of the micro-architecture of a computer (Sperry Univac 1100/60) that generated several billion dollars in revenue and for which he received six patents and a multi-level promotion into senior technical management just two years out of the university. He published many technical articles, chaired two international computer conferences, was the elected chair of the US association of computer architects, and was an invited member of the first delegation of computer experts to tour China in 1978 – before tourist visits were possible for Americans.

Through a series of promotions, Barry progressed (at Unisys) from technical management into general management positions – reaching Group VP and GM of a diversified, multinational business group responsible for thousands of people and hundreds of millions of dollars of revenue. An executive search firm recruited Barry away from Unisys to become CEO of a smaller (less than 200 people) high-tech company. Dr. Borgerson has served on the board of directors of several for-profit and non-profit organizations.

After successfully transforming organizations to new business models and driving the culture changes to implement them, fostering internal entrepreneurial efforts, and developing leaders, Barry felt that the new insights and techniques he gained regarding the impact of automatic human activities offered a breakthrough opportunity for improving performance and sustaining success. To realize this opportunity, he chose to retire from his executive career to concentrate his energies on developing and disseminating this new approach to achieving peak performance.

Dr. Borgerson's theory-based techniques have proven to work effectively in transforming leaders to overcome their barriers to greater performance and to alleviate their counterproductive behavioral patterns permanently. He has coached them to achieve a new level of effectiveness that exceeds what they and those around them had thought possible. This book presents one strand of the concepts and behavior-transformation techniques Barry created over more than a decade and a half.

Table of Contents

Introduction

This book presents fundamental principles that uncover what exists at the deepest core of achieving and sustaining success.

Conquering the Auto-Self

Conquering the auto-self requires that we *recognize* its existence, *understand* how it works, and have the ability to *transform* it when it undermines success. The ability to manage the auto-self systematically creates a new dimension in performance improvement and behavior management.

Recognizing the existence of the auto-self creates new insights into barriers and opportunities for improving personal and organizational effectiveness.

Understanding the details of the auto-self enables us to realize the many ways it affects our success. To our knowledge, this is the first modeling of the automatic mode of human activities in order to create systematic techniques to conquer it. This book presents **principles** that describe the inner workings of the auto-self and **properties** that describe the specific contrasting ways in which the thinking-self and auto-self perform their tasks. These detailed descriptions of the inner-workings of our two selfs established a new theory of human activities that enables us to create techniques to manage human behaviors and performance at a new level.

Transforming the auto-self, which is ultimately the purpose of this book, enables us to overcome debilitating barriers to leveraging our auto-self talents to maximize performance. It also allows us to transform our undesirable or dysfunctional behaviors to avoid derailing our careers or sabotaging our personal relationships.

Create Star Performers

Are you failing to develop the star potential within members of your team?

If you are a manager at any level, your success depends on making as many as possible of your team members star performers. This book will show you how to align their automatic behaviors with the needs of the organization.

Part of leadership entails having a vision of where to take your organization. Other crucial components of leading require that you motivate, hold people accountable for achieving commitments, and develop members of your team. Excelling at those activities requires conquering the auto-self.

Become a Star

Are you neglecting the star potential within you?

This book will enable you to become the star you have always felt you had within you but never quite achieved or restore the star status you once enjoyed. It will empower you to become a star performer at work as well as to achieve your personal goals outside of work.

Self-help efforts to improve undesired behaviors *inherently* produce poor results; we will identify why later.

This book takes you beyond the struggles and pitfalls of self-help because it shows you a powerful new way to reach your fullest potential – a way to enlist a **guide** to support your goals, provide perspective, and redirect your actions. You need not be alone in your efforts to transform and achieve the success you desire.

Be a Star

Definition: **Star Performer**

We use the "star" name and imagery to indicate reaching your peak potential to become a star performer at work and in life. For leaders, star performance includes developing others to perform at their star potential.

Have you ever felt that some people not as smart as you seem to enjoy greater success? Have you ever failed to achieve the results you worked for and don't understand why? Do you experience frustration achieving the level of impact and influence you desire? Do you wish you could methodically improve the effectiveness of people you count on for your success? Do you wonder just what it takes to lead effectively? If so, you are in good company. A significant part of what creates success takes place outside of our awareness and independent of our intentions, intelligence, and technical expertise. **This is the first book to make these previously elusive success factors clearly visible, thoroughly understandable, and methodically manageable**. It provides a roadmap to enable you to achieve your dreams.

For most people, success is not static. At work, success means increasing responsibility, growing accomplishments, and rising compensation. It means reaching the level where you are confident that you are achieving your maximum, while balancing your achievements with family, social, spiritual, health, recreational, and other desired aspects of your life. It means not plateauing before you would like and not having your career derailed.

When most people think of enhancing business success, they think of gaining more knowledge, such as learning new technical material, incorporating new operating procedures, creating new strategies, or getting on a path to continuous improvements. The business community often refers to these attributes as "hard" success factors. They are visible, normally measurable, and *necessary* for success; unfortunately, most people do not realize that hard success factors are *not sufficient*. Other crucial activities, often referred to as "soft" success factors, are not so obvious.

Soft success factors have remained elusive because they are amorphous and usually not measurable. However, they are equally *necessary* for success in business and in life. They also require systematic development.

If you ever wanted to succeed at anything and found that success often eluded you, this book is for you. It can empower you to:

- Elevate the performance of people who report to you beyond what they and those around them believe is possible.
- Align your actions with your goals so that you can achieve nearly anything you want.
- Recognize and stop displaying behaviors that drive people around you crazy.
- Lead and inspire others at work, in your community, and in your family.
- Overcome limiting beliefs about what you can accomplish.
- Achieve those elusive New Year's resolutions.
- Create healthy habits.

Understand and Use Your Mind for a Change

We can no longer afford the complacent practice of ignoring the structure of our mind.

The revolutionary insights and techniques you are about to discover rest on a fundamental and critically important understanding regarding the human mind. A mindset or paradigm that most people use stifles their ability to become star performers or to guide others to become star performers. Most people assume, at least implicitly, that we have a *uniform* mind.

Our Dual Mind

Because we so thoroughly understand how to acquire new knowledge, the next frontier in improving performance lies in creating better ways to understand and improve our automatic activities.

The following illustration represents the prevailing uniform view of the mind, which for most people is informal and implicit.

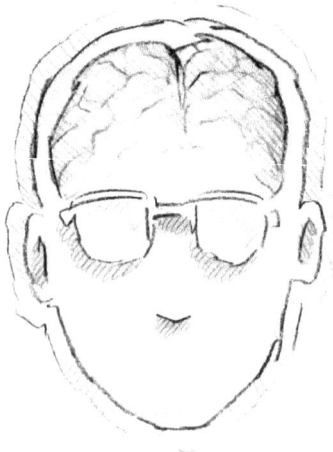

Implicitly Assumed One-Dimensional Mind

In spite of indicators to the contrary in popular books, in business, and in the psychology profession, most people assume that we have a uniform or **one-dimensional mind**. This assumption creates huge barriers to maximizing individual performance and organizational success because it fails to address adequately a second dimension of human activities that determine our successes. If we critically examine the factors that contribute to our successes in life, we discover that we actually operate in two modes. We have a dual or **two-dimensional mind.**

Symbolically, if we were to open up the head of the assumed uniform mind, we would see that inside there are really two independent minds at work as the following image illustrates.

Actual Two-Dimensional Mind

> ## Overarching/Foundational Principle: Humans Have Two "Selfs"
>
> We do not have a *uniform mind* as most people routinely assume. We have a *dual mind* that consists of a thinking dimension and an automatic dimension. These two modes in effect create two distinct "**selfs**" that determine how we act and how we think. We do not have a one-dimensional mind; we have a two-dimensional mind.

When we operate in our cognitive, thinking, knowledgeable mode, we say our *thinking-self* controls our activities. When we display involuntary behaviors, when *paradigms* or *cultures* constrain our thoughts and understanding, we say our *auto-self* controls us. The two modes make up our two "**selfs**" that often work cooperatively but sometimes compete for control of our thoughts and actions.

We now have the mechanism we need to understand why we distinguish so-called "hard" success factors from so-called "soft" success factors and why we have traditionally done so much better managing the former than we have with the latter. Our thinking-self controls the hard success factors. Our auto-self controls the soft success factors. **Once we conquer our auto-self, we will be able to understand and manage the *soft* success factors just as systematically as we now do with *hard* success factors.**

Definition: **Our Two "Selfs"**

We don't speak of having two "selves" because "selves" already means something else – namely the (assumed) *single* "self" of *multiple people* as in "ourselves," "yourselves," and "themselves."

We mean something completely different here. When we use "**selfs**," we refer to the two distinct, simultaneously acting selfs (thinking-self and auto-self) ever-present in each of us.

We also want to avoid the use of "selfs" for describing states associated with some mental aberrations such as bipolar (manic/depressive) episodes, schizophrenia, or dissociative identity disorder (a.k.a. "multiple personality disorder," "split personality").

Our definition of two selfs is consistent with the previously recognized second mode of "unconscious" (Freud) and "subconscious" (pop psychology). However, our auto-self goes much further than these efforts by identifying the *principles* that control the auto-self and the *properties* that describe the inner workings of both selfs.

We use "**selfs**" to focus attention on the *two* distinct but interdependent (sometimes cooperating; often competing for control) selfs constantly present in normal human activities.

Our Familiar Thinking-Self

We cannot miss our thinking-self's activities. Our thoughts are the center of our awareness.

Our thinking-self is the center of our awareness and the source of our intentions and voluntary control. We all spend many years improving this mode during our formal education and beyond. We use this thinking mode to decide our goals, plan how to attain them, and attempt to initiate efforts to achieve these goals. You are using your thinking-self to understand this book. As you will discover, it will take more than using your thinking-self to achieve the improvements presented in this book.

Our Thinking-Self

Definition: **Thinking-Self**

To give it a specific name so we can describe it better, we refer to the thinking mode as the "**thinking-self.**" The thinking-self provides our logic, intentions, goals, consciousness, and voluntary actions that empower us to achieve a specific goal or complete a task. We use the anthropomorphic light bulb to represent the thinking-self.

Our (Previously) Elusive Auto-Self

When you finish this book, the auto-self will no longer be elusive for you. It will be understandable and manageable but completely different from the familiar thinking-self.

Our habitual, robot-like, auto-self actions take place outside of our voluntary control. Our auto-self controls our actions regardless of whether those actions help or hinder our ability to succeed. Unlike the systematic development we apply to our thinking-self, our auto-self receives haphazard development, if anyone tries to develop it at all. Reliably improving the automatic-self requires outside help because we usually do not see our own limiting automatic behaviors (e.g., procrastination; emotional overreactions) and thought patterns (e.g., paradigms; business cultures) and these both tenaciously resist change.

Our Auto-Self

Definitions: **Auto-Self**

To give it a specific name so we can describe it, we refer to the automatic mode as the "**auto-self**." The auto-self is the involuntary internal mechanism that controls aspects of our behavior and thought patterns as if we have a "robot within." We use the anthropomorphic robot to represent the auto-self.

The auto-self is the central theme of this book because it plays a decisive role in our success and because it was previously only implicitly recognized, poorly understood, and haphazardly improved. As such, conquering the auto-self adds a new dimension for improving success.

This book describes a simplified version of a new theory of human activities and how techniques built upon that theory can provide you with a systematic, reliable means to become a star achiever and realize your dreams.

Insight into the existence of two mental modes is not what is new here. Freud studied and wrote about the "unconscious" part of the mind. Popular psychology talks about the "subconscious" mode. Several books indirectly discuss the existence and importance of the automatic mode. In the business-book *Execution: The Discipline of Getting Things Done*, Larry Bossidy and Ram Charan identify what they call the "people process," which encompasses the success factors associated with the auto-self. In the book *Switch: How to Change Things When*

Change Is Hard, Chip and Dan Heath use "elephant" as a metaphor for the automatic mode and "rider" as a metaphor for the thinking mode and they discuss how difficult it is for the rider to move the elephant if the elephant wants to go in a different direction. In *Behavior Change: A View from the Inside Out*, Hank Fieger uses "internal operating system" to identify what we call the auto-self. Another book that provides excellent insights into these two mental modes is *Mindfulness* by Harvard University psychology professor Ellen Langer. She distinguishes the two modes as "mindfulness" (our thinking-self) and "mindlessness" (our auto-self). The business community indirectly discusses the existence of two mental modes when it discusses "hard" success factors to indicate those activities controlled by the thinking-self and refers to activities driven by the auto-self as "soft" success factors.

So, we all "sort of" know we have an automatic or involuntary mode, but neither current formal education nor business training enables us to manage our auto-self well enough to perform at our potential.

This book goes way beyond identifying the existence and impact of our automatic mode. It dramatically extends our understanding of the second mode by expanding the auto-self into a full-blown second dimension of human activities. It identifies many auto-self properties besides the common one that its activities occur outside of our awareness (subconscious). This book presents a theory that describes how automatic activities actually work and builds techniques upon that theory to enable systematic auto-self improvements. Among other things, the two-selfs theory reveals why change is so difficult, why self-help will remain problematic, and how to leverage external resources to create lasting behavioral changes.

If you have ever faltered when attempting to reach a goal or find greater success in your life, most likely your auto-self – the programmed robot-like habitual behaviors, beliefs, attitudes, emotions, and skills – derailed your efforts to succeed.

This book describes the foundational underpinnings of habits and of execution, and it shows how to change undesirable habits and enable consistent execution toward goals. It presents fundamental principles. It uncovers what exists at the deepest core of achieving and sustaining success. *The Auto-Self* will enable you to understand the nature of your automatic mode and how it affects everything you do in your life. This book will also show you how to "reprogram" (with interactive guidance) the "hard-wiring" of your robot-like auto-self to perform at a more powerful level to increase your chances of achieving repeated successes. Conquering the auto-self enables us to penetrate through the next frontier in performance improvement. Understanding and applying the material in this book about the automatic mode of human activities will empower you to ride the next great wave of achieving performance excellence.

However, most people will not create their desired or needed changes on their own because they are not aware of their negative involuntary behaviors, and it takes a systematic life-changing intervention to overcome their interfering or limiting behaviors.

Have you ever known a successful athlete or entertainer who succeeded without a coach or a trainer? Likewise, you are much more likely to achieve your greatest goals in life and at work if you have a personal coach or guide to enable you to transform undesired aspects of your automatic actions.

The two-selfs theory enables us to leverage an understanding of the details and interplay between our thinking-self and auto-self. It explicitly deals with competing priorities between the thinking mode and automatic mode in ways that empower us to overcome the major barriers to positive change. It also leverages the interactions between our thinking-self and our auto-self to create new behavior-change techniques.

The Auto-Self will show you how to make improvements you desire by using a **transformation guide** – a friendly objective supporter who can use the techniques and methods in this book to guide to you succeed at your grandest goals.

Because this book addresses how to overcome stunted potential by making fundamental, lasting improvements to the auto-self, it has a broad audience, including:

- Anyone who has the responsibility to develop others, including managers and HR professionals (and parents!)

- Anyone who has tried to improve themselves through a self-help program and failed to achieve lasting results

- Managers who struggle to *lead* effectively

- People who have not achieved the success they believe they deserve at work

- People who have unhealthy habits, such as overeating, not exercising regularly, or smoking

- People who agonize over someone they care for who is failing to meet his or her potential

- People who lack the self-confidence to achieve in a manner consistent with their intellectual capacity and hard-won knowledge

- Professional transformation coaches who want to acquire new techniques and put a theoretical foundation under some of their current techniques to make them more effective and usable in additional situations

- Academics who would like a acquire new approach to some of their activities, including professors/researchers in business, philosophy of the mind, psychology, and education

Instruction Manual for Our Dual Mind

For maximizing our ability to succeed at work and in life, we have not had an adequate user's manual.

Most "machines" we use come with an instruction manual.

Our automobile comes with a user's manual, which tells us such things as what the lights on the dashboard mean, how to maintain the car properly, and how much air pressure to put in the tires. It does not bother us with details we do not need to care about, such as how the internal combustion engine works or the chemical reactions that create the power in the battery.

Likewise, our laptop computers come with a user's manual that describes such things as how to find files, how to load new applications, and how to use the touchpad. It does not overwhelm us with such details as how integrated circuits work, the inner workings of the magnetic and optical discs, and the details of the construction of the operating system.

For working on mental disorders, psychotherapists have instruction manuals they can use.

For dealing with physical problems of the brain, neuroscientists continuously improve their manual of the structure and functioning of the modules of our brain.

However, for the crucially important task of maximizing our ability to succeed at work and in life, we have not had, until now, an adequate user's manual that includes the automatic dimension of our mind that controls so much of our ability to succeed.

To maximize our performance and sustain success, we do not need an operating manual that tells us about such topics as the neurophysiology of the *brain* or the details of genetic heritability. We need an instruction manual that tells us how our dual *mind* works in a pragmatic sense so that we can consistently execute our success agenda, avoid behaviors that harm ourselves and others, and change the way we see people and situations when our current mindset doesn't serve us well. This book constitutes a pragmatic two-selfs manual on how our dual mind works and how to improve it to maximize our performance and sustain success.

Sidebar: **Mind vs. Brain**

In order to understand and manage automatic human activities at a pragmatic level, we overcome widespread confusion through drawing an explicit distinction between the *mind* and the *brain*. Our **brain** is the 1.4 Kg (3 pounds) of *tangible*, convoluted gray and white matter that resides in our heads. Our **mind** is the *intangible* controller of our realities including our thoughts, knowledge, implicit assumptions, values, emotions, skills, intentions, habits, and behaviors.

When you understand and better manage your habitual behaviors, uncontrollable barriers to action, hidden thought patterns, and business-related reflexive skills (speaking, interpersonal, motivational), you will experience a new exhilaration and a clear view on how to succeed at anything you choose to do.

Who you are today does not have to determine who you will be tomorrow. It is possible to transform deeply ingrained aspects of who you have been. Your potential to succeed is likely much greater than you believe.

Best-practices books are great at leveling the playing field. They help you catch up with the leaders. They aren't designed to help companies or leaders rise ahead of their peers. Techniques based on a breakthrough *new theory*, such as the two-selfs theory described in this book, offer the possibly of leaping ahead of peers and competitors until they catch on and catch up. That possibility becomes a probability when the theory penetrates success factors that were previously recognized but not understood and underpins techniques built upon that new theory that have been tested and verified in practice.

I invite you to take an extraordinary exploratory journey. Besides learning fascinating concepts about the inner-workings of your mind, you will acquire new power to improve the performance of people who report to you. You can also use this book as a manual that someone else can use to guide you to increase your successes at work and in life or you can use to guide friends, colleagues, or family members to do the same. Use this book as your user's how-it-works-and-how–to-improve-it guide to the human mind for maximizing successes.

Part I: Challenges of Changing

If you do not understand and manage your automatic activities, you will never achieve your potential.

Organizations, managers, and HR professionals ignore or neglect the automatic mode to their peril.

1 : **J**ake and Penny Need Help

To help explain the principles and tools discussed in this book, let us look at some common and difficult problems they can help you overcome. See if you recognize challenges in someone who reports to you, in your life, or the life of someone you care for that are similar to those encountered by Jake and Penny.

Jake's Abusive Behavior

"I still believe I don't have a problem." – Jake

Jake knew his company would not promote him to the regional manager position. This was the third time he was passed up and he was not getting any younger. His career, or non-career, was moving forward without him, which frustrated him. He did everything his boss asked in a timely manner, had good performance reviews, and thought he got along with everybody. He could only conclude that his boss didn't like him or that someone in upper management had it in for him. He now felt that he had to leave the job he loved and find something that would advance his career.

However, Jake had done this before. The last job he had as a manager took him only so far. He could not advance to regional manager, so he left the company. He was used to receiving rapid promotions, but then his promotions suddenly stopped as if he had reached the peak of his career. He was depressed. He didn't want to leave his current job; with his oldest daughter about to start college and the expenses growing, advancing his career was imperative.

He decided to check his email and saw a dreaded message from the company HR director, Lori. She wanted to meet with him at 1 pm. He had no idea what this could be about, and could only think of the worst.

After Jake choked down his lunch, he reluctantly went upstairs to Lori's office. When he opened the door, his heart sank. Sitting there was his boss and another man he knew was not an employee of the company. *"I'm being fired!"* he thought.

"Hi, Jake. Have a seat. We have a lot to go over," his boss said.

Assuming the worst, Jake immediately reacted. "How could you do this to me? I've been a loyal employee for six years!" he said, raising his voice.

"Jake, please hear us out. We're trying to help you," Lori said. "Now listen…"

On the defensive, Jake resisted. "I don't know if I want to."

Lori gestured to the seat with a stern look, and Jake finally sat down.

Lori looked at Jake and he seemed to cower – waiting for the expected bad news. Then she spoke, "We want you to have the next open regional manager's position, but the reviews from your direct reports are not good."

Jake was relieved that the company was not firing him, and he managed to create a weak defense. "What do you mean? I've always had good performance reviews."

"Yes, your performance has been extraordinary, but Jake, you're a hard ass."

"Excuse me?"

"A hard ass," Lori repeated. "You don't have enough compassion for your direct reports. You do not give them appropriate slack when they make mistakes or need time off. You don't empathize well with your employees."

"I don't think so," Jake countered. "I always have their needs in mind when making a decision. Haven't our sales doubled since I took over?"

"Yes," Lori acknowledged. "Sales have doubled, but at what cost? Your direct reports are miserable and leave the first chance they get."

Lori raised her hand to hold off a response from Jake. "Haven't you noticed that a lot of your employees put in for transfers to different departments or leave the company? Why do you suppose I rarely find replacements internally when people bail out on you?"

"I don't know," Jake said reluctantly, starting to consider Lori's statements.

"So Jake, we've hired a leadership coach, Cyril, to help you improve your leadership abilities because we really want you to have that regional manager's position. Go through the coaching and let's talk again when it's done."

Feeling ambushed and threatened, Jake turned to Cyril and said, "So you're the expert."

Seizing the opportunity, Cyril, a coach from my company, responded, "Jake, from watching you for the past few minutes, I'll bet that you have issues with getting people to do things for you."

"Ah…I don't know. I get people to do what I tell them."

"Yes, but they probably do it because they have to, not because they want to," Cyril said. "And that means they fail to achieve peak performance. You see, Jake, we base our techniques on a concept that the mind operates in two modes. We all have a thinking, conscious mode and we have an automatic mode that directs our behavior without our knowing it."

"What's that got to do with the price of cheese?" Jake quipped.

"It has a lot to do with your current predicament. Your automatic mode generates your disruptive behaviors. That is why you don't realize you do it. I would also bet that this is not the first time you have been passed over for a promotion."

This assessment seemed to hit home for Jake. His shoulders slumped a bit and he became pensive. After a few moments, he looked up.

"I get done what the company asks of me, using my people."

Jake was still in avoidance mode. Cyril pressed the point further. "Your automatic mode prevents you from being sympathetic because its agenda is to get people to do what you want no matter what the consequences."

Jake thought some more.

"I don't understand what you mean by my automatic mode," he said. "But I still believe I don't have a problem."

"As we go through the coaching process, I will help you understand more about the automatic mode we all have and the impact it has on your success."

"Great. When do we start?" Lori asked.

"We already have," Cyril replied.

Penny's Failures to Achieve Her Dreams

"Nothing I've tried has worked." – Penny

Penny had been divorced for over a year – all for the better, in her mind. Her former husband, she learned later, started cheating on her a month after they were married. She often wondered why he got married in the first place if he wanted to be with other women.

She was over him and now she wanted to find that special someone – someone whom she could trust, who was faithful, and who would love her as much as she would love him. She was ready for a permanent trusting relationship.

She was afraid to try, however, because of a significant challenge – she was 50 pounds overweight. Intuitively, she had suspected her former husband was cheating on her, but she didn't want to believe it. When the evidence became obvious, she would block it out by eating, which was her favorite comfort escape.

Penny was determined to lose the extra weight and find that special someone. She searched the Internet and found several books on "successful" dieting, which she devoured as aggressively as junk food and followed their techniques tenaciously. She joined a gym and exercised as much as possible, but she felt out of place. As she put it, "Most of the people there looked like models out of magazines rather than people struggling with their weight like me."

Penny also tried many other approaches to losing weight. She told a friend, "I have enrolled in dieting courses, dieting programs, and dieting webinars; I've purchased countless CDs, DVDs and self-help programs. I would lose weight but then put it right back on as soon as something frustrated me. After several months, I lost only a few pounds; the main thing I lost was my enthusiasm. "

She decided to call her best friend, Kristen, to ask her for advice. They made a lunch date.

At lunch, Penny talked about her frustration and failure to lose the extra 50 pounds she put on due to her terrible marriage in spite of so many self-help attempts. She told Kristen of all the programs she had read and watched, as well as the countless diets and deprivation of her favorite foods.

Kristen suddenly realized she might have a way to help Penny. "You know, maybe Jeremy can help you."

"You mean your boyfriend Jeremy? How can he help me?"

"Jeremy helped me stop micromanaging at work. I could not seem to stop telling my direct reports how they should do their work, which frustrated them and held me back. My boss was getting frustrated with me."

"Then Jeremy helped me understand that we have two mental modes: one creates the conscious, thinking, planning self; and the other creates an automatic self that regulates our behavior unconsciously. It's that involuntary behavior that causes most of our failures."

"Really? That's interesting."

"Jeremy said I had to reprogram my automatic behaviors so I could get past the micromanaging. I thought he was crazy at first, but he had this whole series of exercises that he put me through, and it helped me discover that I had a fear of failing at work and some really wacky urge to get involved in all of the details instead of trusting my subordinates to handle them."

"How did he know all this stuff?"

"His company retained a transformation coach to help him overcome his anger outbursts at work. Even though he's not an expert coach, he learned enough about the automatic mode from his coach that he has become what he calls a 'transformation guide.' Since he helped me, I'm thinking he could also guide you to establish appropriate health habits to achieve and maintain your desired weight."

"He would do that for me?"

"I bet he would do it happily. He loves it. He's been helping some of his friends, and it's working. They all love what he's done for them."

"Ok," Penny sighed. "At this point, I'll try anything because nothing I've tried has worked. I have tried the famous Corey Banks diet, Weight Reducers, and countless others. I guess self-help doesn't work very well – at least for me."

2: Our Two "Selfs"

Success results not just from what you know but from how you automatically respond to situations.

Jake's and Penny's stories are typical of the automatic mode in action, where involuntary disruptive behaviors or debilitating barriers derail the best intentions without the person even noticing their undesired habits.

Wouldn't it be nice if we could step into someone else's shoes for a while and observe ourselves and everything we do just as others see us? We would clearly see all the things we do poorly – not even knowing we do them – and then we could have a chance to correct our negative or inhibiting behaviors and to get more out of those things we do well.

We rarely notice our automatic activities because habitual behaviors operate outside our normal awareness. However, the proven concepts and techniques in *The Auto-Self* will allow you to recognize and transform your elusive auto-self and set you on the road to greater successes.

Do some of these situations seem familiar to you?

- Have you ever wondered why you procrastinate on certain chores or projects, but are gung-ho and focused on others?

- Do you ever wonder why certain situations, activities, or people make you angry and or why your anger gets the best of you when it emerges?

- Have you ever failed to take a needed action in a confrontational situation when you knew you should take the lead to resolve it?

- Do you ever fail to hold people accountable when they miss a commitment to you?

- How many New Year's resolutions did you enact in the last five years? Would you like to learn why you failed and become able to enact them?

- Have you ever worried about speaking to a large audience even though you have successfully performed this task before?

- Do you ever get frustrated when you point out a counterproductive habit to someone and give up when they don't change because you do not know how to guide them to transform their behavior?

- Have you ever thought about why people have phobias about some things and not others and why they cannot overcome them?

- Do you occasionally find yourself apologizing for a behavior that was contrary to your values and intentions, and not know why you did it?

The answers to these questions likely elude you because the auto-self controls these issues. Our hidden emotions, preconceptions, attitudes, and assumptions cause us to behave in an unintentional manner and sometimes even opposed to our explicit intentions.

We are all familiar with the thinking mode, which processes our thoughts, knowledge, and intellect. The second mode of human actions and thought patterns, which we perform automatically and uncontrollably, has remained elusive to both sound understanding and systematic improvement until now.

We need to conquer the auto-self. Admitting we have this second mode of automatic activities, understanding it, and managing it creates a new and empowering way to improve your success rate at anything you do.

Generally, most people recognize *explicitly*, understand *comprehensively*, and improve *systematically* those success factors associated with their **thinking-self**. After all, most of us spend many years at school and in other activities acquiring knowledge, which is how we improve our thinking-self.

Currently, most people only recognize *implicitly*, understand *poorly*, and improve *haphazardly* the success-determining activities driven by their **auto-self**.

Our "robot within" auto-self gets programmed partially through human nature (our genetic makeup), partly through non-planned environmental pressures, and sometimes through specific social programming, such as when parents condition their children to behave reasonably and when public schools instill patriotism.

Once initially programmed, our auto-self resists change. The major challenge addressed in this book is how "we" (the thinking-self, success oriented, planning aspects of "us") can seize control and reprogram crucial aspects of our auto-self so we can achieve peak performance and the success we want. This is a daunting task because human nature creates potent barriers to auto-self *discovery* and *transformation*.

It is difficult to understand why at this stage of human development we still have such a poor command over our automatic activities. The following table summarizes the vastly different ways we currently handle our two mental modes.

Insight: Our Two Selfs Previously		
Handling Success Drivers		
	Explicit	**Implicit**
Recognizing	Previous: all there is	"Subconscious"
	Future: thinking-self	
Understanding	**Comprehensive**	**Poor**
	Knowledge – "hard"	Metaphoric – "soft"
Improving	**Systematic**	**Haphazard**
	Schooling, college...	Empirical

Previously, the focus was on the thinking-self although we did not view it as such. Now that we can distinguish our thinking-self from our auto-self, we can view the thinking-self with even better understanding as shown by the eight two-selfs properties described later.

With the advent of the two-selfs theory, we make a huge leap in recognizing, understanding, and improving the auto-self. As the following diagram indicates, we now have greatly improved access to the auto-self. In fact, if you compare it with the previous diagram, you will see that we can now handle the success drivers of the auto-self at the same level we handle the thinking-self.

Insight: **Our Auto-Self Emerges**		
Handling Success Drivers	Previous	Two-Selfs Model
Recognizing	**Implicit** "Subconscious"	**Explicit** Auto-self
Understanding	**Poor** Metaphoric – "soft"	**Comprehensive** Descriptive – theory, principles, properties
Improving	**Haphazard** Empirical	**Systematic** Theory-based

There is a strong implicit recognition that we do have an important second mental mode. We discussed some of this recognition in the Introduction, including the "people process," the "elephant," and the "internal operating system." We already discussed how the two-selfs theory enables us to understand and manage what we refer to as "soft" success factors. Likewise, we will understand leadership, leadership development, and the foundational distinction between leadership and management much better when we recognize that the auto-self controls most aspects of leadership and the thinking-self handles most management activities. We *manage things* and we *lead people*.

A New *Dimension* in Performance Improvement

As the following image illustrates, we currently rely mostly on developing the thinking mode when we try to achieve star status. Many organizations do develop some aspects of the automatic mode successfully, such as with leadership and interpersonal skill development. However, the auto-self has stubbornly remained nebulous, so it has evaded systematic development at a level needed for future sustainable success.

Thinking Mode   Automatic Mode
Visible/Manageable   Nebulous/Intractable

Previous
Inadequate Automatic Mode Development

What do we mean when we assert that we now have a new *dimension* of performance improvement and behavior management?

We mean building star performers based on both dimensions of our mental world. We retain the solid improvement abilities for the thinking-self and gain more visibility by revealing some of its *properties*. Now, however, we can make the new dimension of performance achievement, the auto-self, as visible and manageable as the thinking-self. We need both dimensions for star performance.

Thinking-Self   *Auto-Self*
Visible/Manageable   Visible/Manageable

<u>Now</u>
Robust Auto-Self Development
Cooperatively Balanced with the Thinking-Self

Since the general state of recognition of our automatic mode is implicit and through metaphor, we should not expect widespread understanding regarding the auto-self, and there is not. Without a solid understanding, we should not expect to have theory-based systematic techniques to get the most out of ourselves and others, and we do not. The good news is that empirically based leadership development, experiential workshops, and transformational coaching have emerged, which seems to make it unfair to describe our current state of performance improvement as 1-dimensional. To give this perspective, I would describe it as about 1.3-dimensional. That is, full control of the thinking-self and about 30% effectiveness in managing the auto-self. That leaves way too much performance potential untapped. In order to maximize the performance of human resources, we need to use a full-blown 2-dimensional development process. We need to conquer the auto-self.

Sidebar: **Evolution of Our Two Selfs**

The *auto-self* is remote evolutionary development and humans share most of its properties with other animals. The *thinking-self* is a more recent evolutionary development and its properties are unique to humans. Our auto-self creates our "animal" nature. Our thinking-self creates our "uniquely-human" nature. We say our auto-self is "robot-like." We might also say it is "animal-like" since we share properties of our auto-self with other animals. We could call our auto-self our "animal-self," but we want to retain the "auto" (automatic) connotation.

Our robot adds yet another metaphoric pointer to the auto-self. However, we do much more here. We identify properties, or the inner-workings, of the auto-self and that enables us to build systematic techniques, which you will see as you continue reading

Because of this, the automatic mode provides a huge reservoir of potential power that, when tapped properly, creates a torrent of new insights and techniques for improving the previously elusive ("soft") aspects of success.

The auto-self appears in many guises, both in the workplace and in life in general.

The Many Guises of the Auto-Self

The Thinking-Self and Auto-Self Working Together

Imagine you are playing left field on your local baseball team. The batter hits a high fly ball in your direction and now you know it is up to you to catch it. Do you start thinking, "The ball is on a 45 degree trajectory initially traveling at 110 mph toward center field, so I should run 14 feet backward taking large strides, then move left another 20 feet and raise my mitt way over my head so that the ball will land in it?"

No, your auto-self, programmed through practice, automatically guides you regarding how fast to run and where to intercept the ball. (That auto-self ability comes from the co-evolution of predator and prey in our distant evolutionary past.)

As your **auto-self** guides you through the *routine tasks* of intercepting the ball's trajectory and catching it, your **thinking-self** works independently by creating a story to process the *unique situations* of this catch.

"There is a runner on third base, and since there's only one out, I must try to stop him from scoring. However, I am now quite deep in the outfield, so I cannot throw the ball all the way to home plate with enough speed to beat him. As soon as I catch the ball, I will rifle it to the third baseman who will in turn whip it to the catcher."

The same sequence of events happens when you ride a bicycle. You don't think, "I'm turning right so I should lean right or I will not make the turn." Your auto-self does it for you and you don't think about it. Your thinking-self gets involved by deciding where to go.

Driving a car is also an event where both the auto-self and thinking-self work cooperatively to keep the car safely on the road and get you to your destination. You are not thinking, "I have to turn the wheel an inch to the left to move the car 14 feet into the next lane." Again, you just do it without thinking. The thinking-self must read and respond to road signs if you travel to an unfamiliar place.

Our thinking-self, through complex thoughts, handles unique or unusual situations while our auto-self, through imperceptible, automatic processes, simultaneously handles the routine.

The auto-self also appears ubiquitously in the workplace. Have you ever noticed somebody who is very effective at persuading people while somebody else who seems to be smarter and have more knowledge does not do as well? Our thinking-self controls verbal communications using our intelligence and knowledge, but effective communications entails much more. Our auto-self controls our nonverbal communications including gestures, facial expressions, and voice intonation and pace. Nonverbal communication often plays a decisive role, so people who have this auto-skill, either naturally or learned through practice, often persuade effectively.

Road Rage – A Powerful Insight into Our Auto-Self

"Who's in charge here?"

One way to recognize the differences between the thinking and automatic modes is to experience and recognize a conflict between the two. Other people's stories can bore us, but some stories of internal experiences create insights into our own inner workings. Here is a personal story of gaining insight into my automatic mode of behavior. Perhaps this will help you recognize similar internal encounters in your experience.

When I was 20, I noticed that when people cut me off in traffic, I would become enraged, scream at them, and attempt to retaliate by cutting them off as soon as I could. I grew increasingly concerned about my uncontrollable anger and my unsafe retaliatory driving. One day it could either get me an expensive ticket or cause an accident.

Finally, I decided I would no longer react that way when someone drove rudely. When the next person cut me off, how do you think I reacted? ...

I retaliated! After I recovered from losing control, I was flabbergasted, and I was painfully disappointed that I had not done better.

This experience drove me into reality vertigo that made me wonder, "Who's in charge here?" I had created a clear intention to behave differently, yet something "inside me" compelled me to behave badly, as if my intention did not matter. This is similar to the conflict Penny experienced in her quest to lose weight. Although she consciously intended to control her eating, she rarely managed to do it.

I refused to accept my inability to stop my road rage. I resolved that, no matter what, I would not attempt to reciprocate when the next impolite driver aggressively squeezed his or her car between mine and the one in front of me. Since I commuted in city traffic during rush hour, I did not have to wait long for an opportunity to test my resolve. The next time a driver cut me off I did not make aggressive gestures or retaliate.

However, what happened internally astonished me. An almost overwhelming impulse to strike back surged through me. I still felt the driver had trespassed on my rightful territory, and I needed to teach him a lesson. That was the first time I experienced so vividly a struggle between my intentions and my automatic thoughts and actions. It felt like a bewildering internal war over control of my behavior.

This traumatic internal conflict launched an epiphany for me. I suddenly realized I had two distinct aspects of myself competing for control of my thoughts and actions, and "I" didn't have a clue how to control which competitor won.

I learned another valuable lesson during the following months. I continued my determination to avoid retaliatory driving behavior. My internal struggle persisted as my compulsion relentlessly challenged my commitment, but I persevered. After a while, the urge to seek revenge receded.

After a few months, it became comfortable to avoid agitation and to resist retaliation. I overcame my need to strike back by telling myself stories, which was fortuitous because I was two decades away from understanding the automatic, uncontrollable mode and its properties.

I told myself that I was not responsible for reforming rude drivers and that my emotional health, my safety, and the safety of other drivers were more important than avenging someone else's inconsiderate behavior.

Finally, avoiding retaliation became easy for me. In my current terminology, I transformed myself – I became different by reprogramming my auto-self. My new automatic behavior was consistent with my intentions. I no longer had to focus my attention on the problem, and avoiding retaliation no longer required the greatest willpower I could muster.

Sidebar: **Two-Selfs and Multiple Intelligences**

Howard Gardner's theory of multiple intelligences (*Frames Of Mind: The Theory of Multiple Intelligences*) differs widely from Goleman's popular *Emotional Intelligence* – Gardner postulates several different forms of "intelligences" but does not include emotions as one of his intelligences. Our two-selfs theory also postulates multiple types of abilities, but does so in the form of two distinct modes. We view our auto-self's abilities as quite unintelligent – controlled by our robot-like automatic mode. Our thinking-self handles *variational* complexity (like math equations or novels) and our auto-self handles *systematic* complexity (like keyboarding or catching a Frisbee).

Multiple Intelligences vs. Two Selfs

Gardner's Intelligences	Thinking-Self	Auto-Self
Spatial	Handle unique	Natural
Linguistic	Meaning	Structure
Logical-mathematical	Formulas	Relationships
Bodily-kinesthetic	Set goals	Auto-skills
Musical	Read music	Play music
Interpersonal	Verbal	Nonverbal
Intrapersonal	*Observing* auto-self activities	*Detecting* auto-self activities

The road-rage experience convinced me that we have two distinct forces competing for control, that we can *transform* automatic behaviors, and that these new automatic behaviors can endure.

The root cause of many career derailments and corporate failures lies in dysfunctional or inadequate automatic human activities. Explicitly recognizing the existence of this distinct operating mode, understanding how it works, and applying systematic improvement techniques creates the best corrective action for many failures and opens opportunities to achieve greater and more consistent successes.

Definition: **Auto-Behaviors**

Behaviors executed by our auto-self independent of our intentions – for example, our habits, phobias, compulsions, and personality traits.

Auto-behaviors affect our success in two distinct ways – in our ability to execute our success agenda consistently and in our ability to behave non-disruptively.

Insight: **Two Auto-Behaviors Types**

Transformations to improve success come in two distinct types:

- Type 1: *Doing* (Executing) Consistently
- Type 2: *Behaving* Non-Disruptively

Let's take a closer look at the two auto-behavior types to see how they impact our success.

Auto-Behavior Type 1: *Doing* (Executing) Consistently

Knowing is not sufficient; you must also <u>do.</u>

This success attribute seems almost trivial. When you know what to do, do it! But, wait – do you know anyone who sometimes procrastinates? Isn't procrastination failing to take an action that we know will aid our success?

Barriers to Taking Needed Actions:
Brilliance Lacking Execution and Leadership

We can only be star performers if we break down the barriers that keep us from doing what we need to do.

We all know people who fail to execute some of their plans. Most of us sometimes fail to do what we say we want to do and even what we tell others we will do. The culprit is our auto-self. As you will soon learn, our auto-self controls our comfort priorities. When we seek to uncover what keeps us from doing what way say we want to do, we normally discover that something about the task creates discomfort for us. The insidious thing about this process is that we normally do not recognize that discomfort blocks our desired actions. In fact, we usually do not experience the discomfort because we avoid the activity that would create the uncomfortable feelings. The antidote to this poisonous barrier to effective actions is to transform our auto-self to eliminate or at least reduce the discomfort.

**Breaking Through Barriers
to Become a Star Performer**

Jerry's Promotion

Jerry leads the quality assurance department of an engine manufacturing company that operates in a matrix organization. Jerry's intelligence and deep knowledge about his area of responsibility make him very effective at most aspects of his job. However, he routinely failed to attain adequate results from colleagues who did not report to him. Trying to persuade people to execute needed activities created unrecognized discomfort for Jerry. As a result, to his own detriment, he uncontrollably failed to move them to action because he could not meet his commitments if others did not deliver to him on time.

This barrier to action stymied Jerry's career. His previous boss had left the company, and Jerry very much wanted a promotion to his former manager's job. A senior executive in his company told me, "We are not going to promote Jerry and see if he can step up to greater responsibility. Instead, we are going to provide him a coach, and if he learns to perform at a higher level, we will promote him. If he cannot step up, we will hire a new manager for him."

Jerry's management engaged me to coach him to overcome his performance deficit. Jerry summed up his experience with coaching as follows, "When I first entered coaching, I have to say I was skeptical. As I reflect on it, I simply didn't know what I didn't know. I could not understand why the company did not promote me earlier; I thought I was executing extremely well. As I learned to recognize and manage automatic activities that had eluded me, I understood my previous limitations that had blocked my promotion. I was letting barriers to actions undermine my effectiveness in spite of what I thought were my best efforts. I no longer whine to the bosses of people who don't work directly for me that they won't cooperate. I now have a new ability to obtain commitments and to hold people accountable, which enables me to achieve excellent results from people outside of my organization."

When we started our coaching engagement, Jerry was so skeptical that he bet me a dinner that the company would not promote him before our one-year coaching program ended.

Shortly before our coaching engagement concluded, Jerry received the promotion he longed for but had feared he would never achieve. Jerry happily bought me the dinner to pay off his bet and to celebrate his promotion, and he enthusiastically told me, "This process worked so well for me that I now use it on people who report to me. When they come to me complaining that they can't get actions from people outside our organization, I apply some techniques you used on me and send them out to try again." Jerry now works effectively as a transformation guide for members of his team. He leads them and he develops them.

Similarly, Penny suffered from debilitating barriers with regard to her weight management. That is why she needed the support of a transformation guide to enable her to change her auto-behaviors regarding eating and exercising.

Johnnie's Dread of Not Being Liked

Some people are so much in need of having everybody like them that they become unable to make tough decisions. Johnnie was a client who exhibited this characteristic. He had been a high-level staff person reporting to the COO of a large corporation. He sought and was given a line role in an effort to launch a new career path. In this case, I was overseeing another coach from my organization who was coaching Johnnie. One of the exercises we take clients through is to list those aspects of themselves they would like to change and those aspects of themselves they do not want to change. Among those characteristics that Johnnie listed that he did not want to change was any aspect of his personality. We understood this, because he has a most pleasing personality and we did not notice any undesired behaviors. That served him very well when he was doing staff work using the authority of the powerful COO whom he was representing. However, we challenged Johnnie on his lack of desire to make a fundamental change in his personality. He was not limited by errors of *commission* but rather by errors of *omission*.

Johnnie was not going to succeed in his new line responsibility if he did not transform himself beyond his uncontrollable need for having everybody like him. One of the transformations we guided Johnnie through was to switch his guiding principle from having people *like* him to having them *respect* him. That transformation enabled him to go from a nice-guy staff person to a more tough-minded line executive. If you are highly respected, most people will actually like you. However, you should not have that as your goal. We emphasize fairness in making tough decisions and using assertiveness as opposed to aggressiveness. With the help of his coach, Johnnie successfully navigated through this and other transformations with excellent results. He now leads a department with many professionals spread around the globe.

Auto-Behavior Type 2: *Behaving* Non-Disruptively

It's not just what you do but how you do it that creates sustained success.

Aggressive leaders often achieve short-term results but normally at the devastating price of undermining long-term success. Dominators rely on fear as an external motivator and are satisfied with gaining grudging compliance instead of eliciting much more effective internal motivations of enthusiasm, energy, and commitment. Angry, intimidating, and micromanaging behaviors sap the energy and creativity from the recipients of these counterproductive behaviors. The collateral damage these leaders create often overwhelms the benefits of their own results-driven activities. The days when boards hire and celebrate infamous CEOs like "Chainsaw" Al Dunlap are ending. Dunlap devastated Sunbeam, but other less dramatic examples still play out in many organizations. I have coached many smart, hard-driving, results-oriented leaders who executed most aspects of their jobs excellently but won the prize as the CDO (Chief Demotivational Officer).

It is a common business axiom that it's not just what you do but how you do it that counts. CDOs repeatedly de-motivate those around them — sometimes driving valuable employees out of the organization because star performers don't have to tolerate aggressive behavior. CDOs operate like vacuum cleaners; but instead of sucking unwanted dirt and dust off the floor, they suck crucial drive and creativity out of everyone around them.

Inadequate Leader: Executing but Demotivating

We must consistently "do," or execute, the tasks needed to achieve success. However, to succeed in the long run, leaders must temper execution with behaving in ways that do not create personal success at the expense of others and therefore of their company.

> Insight: **Managing and Leading**
>
> Remember: we *manage things* and we *lead people.*
>
> People who execute but demotivate *manage well* but *do not lead effectively.*
>
> **Star leaders** do the opposite – they motivate those around them. They *manage well* and *lead effectively.*

When leaders with disruptive behaviors transform to avoid such counterproductive habits, they do not create stars automatically of everyone around them. However, as illustrated in the following drawing, they restore the "starness" ability to others so that they can now reach for their potential without getting undermined by the disruptive leader. Star leaders also develop their team members so they become stars.

Star Leader: Executing and Motivating

Moderating George's Excesses

George, a senior manager in a manufacturing company, has no blockages to getting into action. In fact, he is all action. However, he used to think so poorly of others who did not share his drive that he would become enraged and aggressive when they did not meet the high standards he set for them and himself. This caused colleagues and subordinates to avoid contact with him whenever they could. Far from spurring greater action, aggressive behavior blocks the creativity and drains the energy from those exposed to it. Although repeatedly warned to rein in his dysfunctional behaviors, George made little headway. Self-help to overcome aggressiveness rarely produces the desired results. To capitalize on his deep knowledge and consistent execution, his company engaged me to coach George to curtail his overbearing behaviors. Within a few weeks, colleagues began to notice and comment on how pleasurable it had become to work with George. For the first time, others could appreciate his outstanding talents and value to the company. Although it takes a long time – we usually plan for a year – to make these changes permanent, some behavior change normally becomes evident quickly.

Fortunately, once people recognize how much their behavior demotivates others and lowers their sustained output, they can change successfully through coaching. For long-term success, leaders must focus not only on achieving results but also on how they achieve those results.

In our continuing narrative of Jake, he displayed disruptive behaviors that he failed to recognize, and this leadership deficiency kept his organization from achieving even greater success; it also stalled Jake's career growth.

Both doing consistently and behaving non-disruptively are examples of the *auto-behavior* mechanism of the auto-self. Thus, in business and life in general, success falters when we fail to execute needed actions or we behave in ways that adversely affect those around us. We maximize our success and ultimately our happiness when we overcome any uncontrollable performance deficits and behavior excesses.

Insight:
Conquering the Automatic Dimension

Conquering the automatic dimension means gaining control of this mode of human activities so that we can maximize performance two-dimensionally.

Explicit recognition: Increased success requires we jettison the pathetically weak metaphor of "soft" success factors. We need to identify this second dimension explicitly so we can describe it. We have named this performance-achievement dimension the "auto-self."

Detailed description: We need to describe how the auto-self works so we can understand it and predict how it will react to external interventions. The *principles* that describe auto-self activities and the *properties* that describe the interplay between the auto-self and thinking-self create a 2-selfs theory that enables us to build powerful intervention techniques.

Systematic improvement: Many empirically derived improvement techniques, honed through trial and error, produce good results. We can use all of these and more when we use theory-based techniques. Additionally, we can extend existing techniques to new situations.

Conquering the auto-self enables us to identify situations where it needs improvement, understand how it works, and reliably transform undesired behaviors, overcome a debilitating barriers to execution, and leverage our auto-self talents.

Mick's Story – When Intentions Fail

"My bullying behavior controlled me; I could not control it." – Mick

Mick is the third-generation CEO of a family-owned mid-size automotive supply company. His intelligence, technical expertise, and business acumen all enabled him to excelling at managing the measurable aspects of his company, but he faltered when it came to leading his employees.

"I could perform most of my activities well, but I couldn't control my temper," he explained. "When anyone screwed up, I exploded and attacked them – often humiliating them in public."

"My HR Director persuaded me that my behavior was sapping my employees' energy and undermining their creativity, so I decided to change. What a traumatic experience! Sometimes I did not even notice my aggressive behavior. When I did notice, I still could not control my rages. My bullying behavior controlled me; I could not control it."

We return to Mick later, after introducing some transformation techniques, to show how I coached him thorough his disruptive behaviors.

Mick's story is similar to many people's attempts to fix what they know is negative or detrimental behavior, but who fail miserably. Penny's weight management difficulties demonstrated another example, and failed New Year's resolutions provide ubiquitous examples.

If you lead an organization or otherwise have responsibilities for the performance of others, you probably have encountered "Micks" that you would like to improve.

You likely have told them that they need to change. Unfortunately, people usually cannot transform their auto-self *characteristics* on their own.

Definition: **Auto-Self *Characteristics***

We refer to the profile of individuals' specific automatic behaviors, thought patterns, and skills as their auto-self *characteristics*. In this book, we focus on **auto-behavior** *characteristics*.

It's difficult to help other people change without understanding the nature of the underlying mental processes that drive uncontrollable behaviors and thought patterns.

This is where one needs a *transformation guide,* in the form of a trusted friend, colleague, of family member, who actively commits to helping the person "reprogram" their troubling automatic behaviors into enabling behaviors. If the trusted guide cannot help, then one may need the services of a professional leadership or behavior-change coach.

Sidebar: **Swiss Army Knife or Blank Slate?**

Philosophers argue circularly about the superiority of the "computational" (or "blank slate") versus "Swiss Army knife" architectures of the mind.

Philosopher Jerry Fodor highlights the problem while critiquing the "massively modular" model of the mind (*London Review of Books*, Vol. 20, No. 2, 22 January 1998).

"For, eventually the mind has to integrate the results of all those modular computations and I don't see how there could be a module for doing that. The moon looks bigger when it's on the horizon; but I know perfectly well it's not. My visual perception module gets fooled, but I don't. The question is: who is this I? And by what – presumably global – computational process does it use what I know about the astronomical facts to correct the misleading appearances that my visual perception module insists on computing? If, in short, there is a community of computers living in my head, there had also better be somebody who is in charge; and, by God, it had better be me."

Our two-selfs theory solves Fodor's dilemma. Our auto-self acts as specialized processors (like blades in the "Swiss Army knife") to process the moon's image and present it to our thinking-self where our attention lies. Our thinking-self, which behaves like the "computational" model of the mind, processes our rational information and is easily capable of understanding that the atmosphere magnifies the size of the image we see when the moon is low on the horizon.

Auto-Contexts

We view our internal and external worlds through internally constructed "lenses."

You probably have noticed how hard it is to enact a paradigm shift, think outside the box, or change a culture. These are examples of how auto-contexts affect success at work.

Definition: **Auto-Contexts**

Auto-contexts are assumptions hidden in the auto-self that frame our realities. They create a "lens" through which we interpret our realities. These framings appear to us not as something constructed by our environment but as the way things "really are."

Examples of auto-contexts include company business models, attitudes, the viability of science, and self-images. We sometimes refer to these "lenses" as "paradigms," "the box," "mental models," "mindsets," and, when shared, "cultures."

Jake provides an excellent example of an inability to make a needed auto-context switch so he can change his self-image about some of his leadership abilities.

Sidebar: **Auto-Contexts**

Auto-contexts serve us well by establishing a stable framework to interpret mass amounts of sensory inputs. When shared with others, auto-contexts provide a consistent framework in which to communicate. This contextual stability works well for us when our environment stays fairly constant. However, when our environment changes dramatically, the stability benefit becomes a liability. That is why we find it so hard to create new scientific theories, to react quickly when new competition emerges, and to alter our self-image when it blocks our willingness to change. We acknowledge this difficulty in reconstructing auto-contexts when we speak of the elusiveness of paradigm shifts, how difficult it is to think "outside the box," and "culture lock."

Four Ways the Auto-Self Impacts Our Success

The auto-self affects success beyond involuntary behaviors.

The auto-self encompasses not only one's behaviors, but also a collection of feelings, hidden rules, skills, and pattern recognition abilities that have been formed over one's lifetime. It is a breakthrough to recognize that the auto-self affects our success in four distinct ways.

Principle: **Auto-Self Impacts Success 4 Ways**

1. **Auto-Behaviors:** No thinking – involuntary, habitual behaviors
2. **Auto-Contexts:** Hidden assumptions about the way things really are (paradigms, the "box," cultures)
3. **Auto-Skills:** Activities automatically repeated
4. **Auto-Expertise:** Pattern and relationship recognition

While all four of these distinct auto-self mechanisms play crucial roles in our success, **this book focuses on the impact of our auto-behaviors in achieving our success agenda** in the form of our goals, our dreams, our aspirations, and our hopes. The next book in the 2-Selfs Series will focus on *auto-contexts* and the crucial role they play in individual and organizational success.

3: Reconciling Dual Priorities

*The greatest impediment to peak performance comes from **comfort priorities** (pleasure that compels; discomfort that repels) that imperceptibly interfere with **success priorities**.*

When we repeatedly fail to enact an intention, we have a hidden discomfort – often unacknowledged and unnoticed.

The auto-self and the thinking-self use fundamentally different mechanisms to control our activities. When these two mechanisms drive us in the same direction, we have aligned priorities, and success normally follows.

However, when these priorities oppose each other, we end up encountering dueling dual priorities – the cause of many failures.

Principle: **Dual Priorities**

Two distinct forces control our actions and therefore we have two types of priorities:

- **Success Priorities**: Our thinking-self creates our *success priorities* through intentions in the form of strategies, goals, plans, and task lists.
- **Comfort Priorities**: Our auto-self creates our *comfort priorities* that compel us to seek pleasure and repel us from accepting discomfort.

The key to managing our success is to ensure that both the auto-self and thinking-self have the same priorities and that they work harmoniously toward achieving important goals. Managing the dual priorities of these two modes creates consistent performance toward sustained success.

Success Priorities

"Success is a personal standard – reaching for the highest that is in us – becoming all that we can be."
– Zig Ziglar

Our Thinking-Self Creates Our Success Priorities

Our thinking-self establishes our success priorities because we have learned through knowledge what we need to do to succeed.

Professional people normally spend many years learning the information and processes associated with their field or profession.

Tradespeople similarly spend considerable time learning techniques to perform well at jobs such as electricians, plumbers, or roofers.

People use their knowledge to design, manufacture, repair, market, or measure results. They translate broad knowledge into results through strategies, goals, plans, and task lists. It seems straightforward and easy enough. Unfortunately, it does not always work out as easily as it sounds.

Comfort Priorities

"Success is not the key to happiness. Happiness is the key to success. If you love what you are doing, you will be successful." – Albert Schweitzer

Our Auto-Self Creates Our Comfort Priorities

We have a second, independent driving force that competes for control of our actions and thought patterns – our *comfort priorities*, which relentlessly repel us from accomplishing uncomfortable tasks no matter how important they are to our success. Comfort priorities also seductively beckon us to devote time and energy to pleasurable activities that may have nothing to do with achieving success or that may actually undermine our success. Our robot-like comfort priorities operate independently from our success priorities because our auto-self controls our comfort priorities.

Aligned Priorities

"To be successful, you have to have your heart in your business and your business in your heart."
– Thomas Watson, Sr.

Winning When Success and Comfort Priorities Align

When our comfort priorities align with our success priorities, successes result because we take pleasure and comfort from the conditions, choices, and actions that result in success.

Competing Priorities

"Nothing can stop the man [or woman] with the right mental attitude from achieving his [or her] goal; nothing on earth can help the [woman or] man with the wrong mental attitude." – Thomas Jefferson

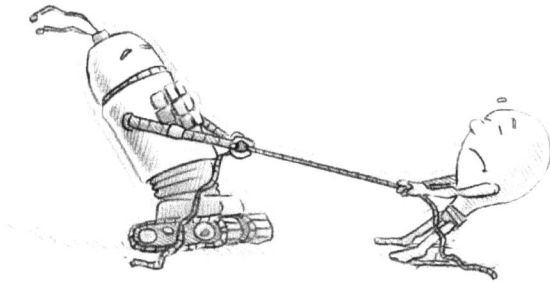

Trouble When Success and Comfort Priorities Compete

When our comfort priorities compete with our success priorities, failure looms. When focusing on our success priorities, we must remain ever vigilant of our "robot within" that may drive comfort priorities that undermine our success. In her quest to lose weight, Penny succumbed to the comfort priorities of her auto-self and subsequently could not reach her goal.

A major goal of auto-behavior transformations and auto-context reconstructions is to transform dueling priorities into cooperating priorities.

Habit-change coaching closes the knowing/doing gap by aligning comfort priorities with success priorities. We align what you feel like doing and don't feel like doing with what you think you should do and shouldn't do to succeed.

Bruce's Transformation

"It horrifies me to discover at this stage of my career how much of my success has been accidental."
– Bruce

Bruce, the CFO of $100 million West Coast industrial manufacturing company, relied too much on his own technical excellence and did not develop his team sufficiently.

Although his company required annual performance reviews, Bruce avoided them, or when pressured, provided superficial reviews.

I asked him about the feedback he had given to members of his team and his satisfaction with their overall performance.

"I prefer the indirect way to improve their performance rather than devastating them by ramming their deficiencies down their throats. I sent them to technical and leadership training seminars, and although I have seen improvements, some of them still are not performing at the level I need."

Bruce misunderstood why he was not giving adequate performance reviews. Fortunately, Bruce decided to engage a coach for other issues, and during his coaching activities, he soon recognized how he had been fooling himself about why he did not provide candid performance reviews.

Here's how Bruce, with some embarrassment, described his new insight, "I thought I was protecting my employees. Actually, I was depriving them of the frank, constructive feedback they needed to overcome their deficiencies and create new proficiencies. I finally understood that my own discomfort at providing corrective feedback blocked my needed actions. I thought I was giving real reasons when I claimed I was protecting them. I now understand I was just rationalizing by giving feeble excuses because I couldn't overcome my own discomfort."

Bruce failed to take needed developmental actions with his direct reports because he had competing internal priorities. His success priorities, controlled by his thinking-self, dictated he should give feedback to his employees that would help them grow; but his comfort priorities, driven by his auto-self, repeatedly blocked those needed actions. To avoid further discomfort by acknowledging he was failing to take needed actions, he rationalized his actions (an "evasion gimmick" that we will discuss later) – he told himself he was acting compassionately when he avoided giving them honest and constructive feedback.

Bruce looked at other automatic activities that were hampering his performance and lowering the performance of his team, and he went on to transform the critical ones.

"It horrifies me to discover at this stage of my career how much of my success has been accidental," he told me. "Some of my involuntary activities, including my assertiveness and energy, served me well, but others, such as my inability to make unpopular decisions or to resolve conflicts quickly, were increasingly lowering my effectiveness."

"Discovering the existence and nature of the auto-self has created a major transformation in my professional and personal life. I have known for a long time that we poorly understand many success factors in business, including leadership, internal motivation, procrastination, and other so-called 'soft' issues. I read books and attended seminars to learn how to manage these elusive issues, and I think I made some progress. However, it always seemed that I was viewing this topic through a foggy lens. Now I understand this other dimension of succeeding and thanks to what I learned in my coaching, I have some explicit tools for conquering it."

Bruce then started to connect the dots with concepts he learned from the literature. He observed that in their excellent book, *Execution: The Discipline of Getting Things Done*, Larry Bossidy and Ram Charan identify what they call the "people process" that seems to encompass what others call "soft success factors." They state that the people process is not an intellectual exercise. Then, they give many examples of problems associated with the people process – including emotional blockage, micromanaging, attitude change, inability to act decisively, and behaviors that drain others. However, they never seem to get to the foundation of what aspect of human nature controls these processes nor do they give organized techniques for managing them.

These wise, experienced authors assert, "The people process is more important than either the strategy or operations processes." Even with the little bit Bruce knew about the two-selfs theory, he began to understand that the thinking-self controls most of the strategy and operations processes (and therefore our explicit success priorities) while the auto-self controls the people process (and therefore our comfort priorities). This makes the auto-self and our comfort priorities of paramount importance for effective execution in the workplace (and in our personal lives!).

Bruce got it. He connected what he learned and experienced in his coaching activity to troubling issues that had eluded him in the past and to some aspects in the business literature. The authors of *Execution* also claim, "If you don't get the people process right, you will never fulfill the potential of your business." Using the two-selfs theory we describe in this book, we could paraphrase their quote as follows "If you don't get the comfort priorities right, you will never fulfill the potential of your business." Bruce leveraged his new insight to make still greater improvements within his organization.

"Now that I understand this automatic mode of activities, I lead more effectively by changing my own counterproductive auto-self characteristics. I also have helped my team members to overcome some undesirable aspects of their automatic modes. I intend to continue to help them improve; if I fail to help them transform some of their involuntary behaviors, I know I can always bring in a professional coach to make that happen."

"I have more confidence now that I have control of the levers of my own performance as well as the success of my finance department. Oh yes, as a serendipitous byproduct, I now understand the behavior of my teenagers better and I am taking actions to help them grow into adulthood more effectively."

Like Jerry (the quality assurance director) and Jeremy (the friend who agreed to guide Penny), Bruce leveraged his coaching experience to become an effective transformation guide. Regardless of whether you receive professional coaching that you can leverage to become a guide, the insights and techniques in this book will enable you to guide others.

The Power of Comfort Priorities

Our thinking-self cannot overpower strong comfort priorities by sheer force of will.

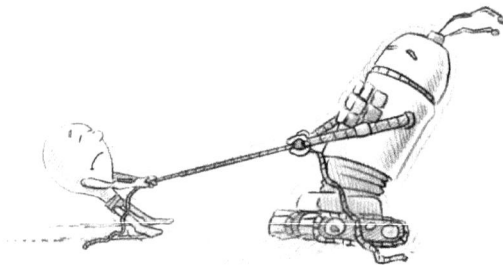

Comfort Priorities Often Overwhelm Success Priorities

Our environment, our goals, and our values create our path to succeed.

Sometimes our comfort priorities do not create strong feelings, so we can blast through them when they oppose our success agenda, such as when we give up a favorite TV show to study for a course or do an unpleasant chore.

However, many times our comfort priorities create a compelling driving force that we must deal with immediately. Powerful comfort drives repel and compel us whether we like it or not.

Our thinking-self cannot, by sheer force of will, *overpower* strong comfort priorities. Instead, we must create other feelings that *counteract* the effects of comfort priorities that oppose our success priorities. Errant comfort priorities can create a merciless driving force that people ignore or reject to their peril.

A leader once sternly told me, "I do not have feelings." This person was very intense, totally driven to succeed, obnoxiously rude to people he thought did not execute effectively, and passionately resistant to acknowledging his strong feelings.

Some leaders, particularly those in manufacturing, quality assurance, and accounting, claim feelings have no relevancy to business. In their opinion, business must run only by the numbers. These people mistakenly believe they can decide the impact that feelings have on business success. They can deny they have feelings or claim that feelings don't affect business success, but that does not change human nature or the power of comfort priorities and their effects.

Their opinions cannot change the fact that avoiding discomfort blocks some needed actions and that seeking pleasure often creates counterproductive behaviors.

Sidebar: **Two-Selfs and Emotional Intelligence**

Daniel Goleman's formulation of Emotional Intelligence (*Emotional Intelligence: Why It Can Matter More Than IQ*) and our concept of comfort priorities deal with similar issues but in a different way. Goleman sees our emotions as controlling us through some type of intelligence. We see comfort priorities as driving us through robot-like auto-self processes that we must reprogram (transform) to improve. Goleman focuses on the brain (amygdala, prefrontal cortex…) while we focus exclusively on the mind (thinking-self, auto-self, intentions, dual priorities …). Goleman's work provided a great service by making what used to be a dreaded four-letter "f" word now acceptable for discussion in polite society and in business – "f-e-e-l."

The two-selfs theory also addresses automatic activities not associated with emotions or feelings – for example, automatic skills, expertise (holistically seeing patterns and relationships), and auto-contexts.

4: Internal Reality Wars

When we try to change a habit or auto-context, we usually experience painful internal reality wars.

Penny, Mick, and I experienced what we call internal reality wars when we unavoidably encountered two forces pulling us in different directions. Jake has not experienced this tug of war yet because he refuses to accept that he has a problem with his leadership skills. The concept of internal struggles between competing realities appeared powerfully in the seminal book, *Theory of Cognitive Dissonance*, by Leon Festinger.

My road-rage story that I described earlier provides a graphic example. I had my thinking-self success priority – my decision that I was not going to engage in road rage – and I had my auto-self comfort priority that was impelling me to avoid my discomfort by acting out and teaching those rude drivers a lesson. I experienced a traumatic reality war between these two internal driving forces when I decided to stop driving outrageously.

> ## Definition: **Internal Reality Wars**
>
> The internal conflict we experience when we encounter two opposing realities. For example, we encounter an internal reality war when a 360° performance survey contradicts our self-image. Our comfort priorities involuntarily drive us to escape the conflict.

When we try to change a habit or auto-context, we usually experience painful internal reality wars. Try to re-experience what it felt like if you tried to quit smoking, avoid indulgent eating, exercise regularly to improve your health, or give corrective feedback to one of your subordinates. You no doubt experienced reality wars between your success priorities – your intention to change – and your comfort priorities associated with overeating, smoking, sedentary behavior, or avoiding giving critical feedback to members of your team.

Have you ever tried to stop an annoying habit using a New Year's resolution or a promise at home or at work? If so, I suspect you can re-experience the personal reality wars you faced, whether you succeeded or not. You may have experienced frustration, anxiety, feelings of defeat, or bad moods when you fought these internal reality wars.

Besides the reality wars associated with changing habits, we also have thought-based internal reality wars. A mild form occurs when two people provide contradictory assertions as "expert" witnesses in trials.

Much more disturbing internal reality wars occur when information from the outside world challenges our beliefs or fundamental assumptions embedded in our auto-contexts. This happens, for example, when we encounter information that contradicts our self-image, someone we trust lying to us, the death of a loved one, or the looming failure of our business plan.

Internal reality wars inherently create discomfort. Most attempts at fundamental change create internal reality wars and therefore discomfort, which is the fundamental reason most people give up on the change process, including to stop procrastinating on important actions and to stop displaying undesired behaviors, if they do not have external help.

Penny's Internal Reality Wars

"Shoulda, coulda, woulda." – Penny

It was the start of a new day in early spring several months before she met Jeremy, the transformation guide, whom her friend Kristen introduced to her. Penny's alarm clock was buzzing. She opened her eyes and was feeling good about everything – she had not slept that well in months.

She looked in her closet and decided to wear her new designer jeans with the flowered pockets that she purchased on sale the previous fall. She showered, put on the brand new pants, pulled them up, and found she could not bring the zipper all the way up.

"These fit perfectly last fall. Did I gain that much weight?" she thought. Her day was turning darker.

She stepped onto her white bathroom scale and glanced down at the number. Her heart sank. She realized that she had gained an additional 10 pounds since last fall, and now she could not squeeze into her favorite jeans.

"I've got to lose weight," she thought, "and right away."

On the way to work, Penny drove so recklessly that she nearly caused an accident twice. She was angry and disappointed with herself for gaining ten additional pounds. It was not what she wanted. She had tried to lose weight all along. Now she couldn't wait to get to work at the post office and talk to Samantha, who worked at the customer-facing station and who lost quite a bit of weight in the past few months.

It was busy that morning at the post office and Penny could not talk to Samantha right away. Her frustration grew.

Later, she waited in the break room a few minutes before Samantha took her break.

"Hi, Sam. You look great!" Penny said rushing towards the middle-aged woman as she entered. "I wanted to ask you what diet you were on to lose all that weight."

"Hi. You will just love it! I could eat what I wanted and I still lost the weight. It's the Corey Banks diet. You order a monthly meal plan, follow their exercise regimen, and stay away from the list of "No No" foods and it works. I lost about three pounds a week."

"Exercise?" Penny's face soured. "Gosh, I'm exhausted when I get home."

"It's not that bad. Fifteen minutes a day. They give you a DVD to follow."

"Oh."

Samantha dug into her purse and pulled out a coupon.

"Here, use this to sign up. You can go to their website or call the 800 number. Make sure you put in my code number so I can get a discount on my next order. You will get a free week of meals using the code."

"Is it expensive?"

"Depends what you order and you can pay weekly."

"Thank you so much." Penny hugged Samantha and went back to work feeling relieved, happy, and burden free.

That evening Penny called the 800 number on the coupon and ordered the diet program. The day did not turn out so bad after all, she thought.

Three weeks later, Penny awoke to her alarm energized and ready for her day because she was supposed to have lost nine pounds.

She stepped on the scale and she saw that she lost only one pound! Again, she was angry with herself, disappointed and instantly in a bad mood.

"I should have put more into the exercise program. I shouldn't have cheated a few times thinking it wouldn't matter," she thought. "Maybe this diet doesn't work after all. Maybe Samantha was lying. Shoulda, coulda, woulda."

Her internal reality war was in full swing again. She had strong desire and solid determination to lose weight and keep it off, but she also had what she called, "something inside me that drives me to eat things I know I shouldn't and fail to exercise when I know I should." Penny's struggle is typical of what people encounter when they try to change undesired habits – an internal reality war between desires and intentions of the thinking-self warring with compelling and repelling drives of the auto-self. She felt terrible, disappointed, and frustrated. She had one more week left of the food she ordered from the Corey Banks diet. If she did not lose more than a few pounds by next week, she was giving up on Corey Banks, she decided. Besides, she hated the exercise. It was just too painful. Stay tuned for the solution to her dilemma.

5: Evasion Gimmicks

You cannot evade/avoid your way to success.

When Coping Mechanisms Backfire

When we inadvertently use evasion gimmicks, we unfortunately engage in self-sabotage.

Life sometimes imposes difficulties on us. To handle the discomfort of setbacks, we have several mechanisms that we can use to cope with bad breaks or personal failures.

A friend of mine displayed this mechanism when he lost his job. He told me he was not happy in the job anyway and this was probably a good time to move on to find something better. He had just suffered a setback that he could not reverse. Telling himself a rationalization story was beneficial. It helped him cope with the serious discomfort of losing his job. However, the same coping mechanism backfires when we use it to rationalize why we are not taking actions that determine our success.

Principle: **Evasion Gimmicks**

When we encounter something that creates discomfort
for us, our comfort priorities relentlessly drive us to
evade the discomfort. Since most auto-behavior
transformations create discomfort, we blindly try to
escape the conflict. Since noticing that we are failing
to make the behavior changes we desired would also
create discomfort, we use evasion gimmicks, or mental
tricks, to avoid noticing. This insidious mechanism
derails most self-help efforts.

Instead of facing and dealing with the issues that
blocked his previous promotions, Jake reacted this way:

"I get the feeling they really don't recognize what I did
for the company. Well, if I don't get this regional manager's
position, I'm leaving and it will be their loss."

Penny robbed herself of the energy to engage effectively
in the change process when she rationalized:

"I really didn't think it was a good diet anyway. I'm
sorry I wasted my time on this one, and I know there are
better ones out there."

We unconsciously and tenaciously strive to escape
internal reality wars. Sometimes these private reality wars
signal us that we need to change an auto-behavior (e.g.,
curtail anger outbursts or overcome procrastination) or
reconstruct an auto-context (e.g., change a counter-

productive attitude or recalibrate an unrealistic self-image) to align with our success needs.

We know (thinking-self) we have to make a change (success priorities), but these self-imposed transformations on our auto-self inherently create discomfort, and we resort to mental tricks to resolve the internal conflicts and end up abandoning our success priorities.

The comfort priorities operate insidiously because we do not normally notice the process, and we have clever ways of evading the discomfort without noticing the consequences.

Although the comfort drives often cause our failures, they also should prevent us from allowing ourselves to fail. That is, if we understood we were making a poor choice based on unnecessary or harmful actions or inactions, then the resulting discomfort should force us to take more-constructive actions.

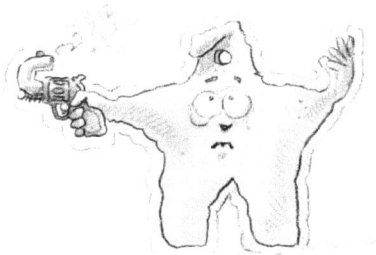

Evasion Gimmicks Backfire

How then do we avoid noticing when our comfort priorities drive us into activities that are contrary to our success needs? To evade discomfort, we use clever, but often dysfunctional, gimmicks (mental tricks) to avoid noticing when we display undesired behaviors or fail to take needed actions.

When we inadvertently use these "**evasion gimmicks**," we unfortunately engage in self-sabotage. Evasion gimmicks backfire on us. We avoid short-term discomfort, but often at the expense of achieving or sustaining success.

Following are some common **evasion gimmicks** used by most people. As you read this list, try to identify ones you have used recently. After you recognize the different forms of evasion tactics, try to notice when you use them in the future. Also, if you want to perform transformation guidance for friends or colleagues, look for and expose the evasion mechanisms that they use.

As you guide someone, that person will reflexively and persistently try to use evasion gimmicks to avoid the discomfort intrinsic to transformational change. One of the primary benefits a transformation guide provides is to unmask the use of evasion gimmicks. This strips away the self-deception inherent in evasion gimmicks and forces people to face their issues.

Rationalization

You cannot rationalize your way to success.

With this evasion gimmick, people tell themselves that the task was not important so it is all right to skip it. Unfortunately, they often use rationalizations counter-productively to escape an internal reality war caused by knowing they are failing to take an action needed for their success.

Here is how Penny would blow off the importance of exercise: "I know exercise is important, but I've joined a gym and only felt like a freak there. I have tried to exercise on my own, but I just cannot seem to drag myself out there. Besides, I don't know what the right exercise is for me. I don't really have to exercise now that I'm on this new super diet program."

Jake would rationalize that when an employee left his team, the employee was not good enough anyway. In fact, many were star performers and left because of his obnoxious behavior.

Bruce, the CFO we discussed earlier, avoided the discomfort associated with failing to help his team improve by rationalizing that he was showing compassion when he failed to give developmental performance reviews.

Procrastination

You cannot procrastinate your way to success.

People acknowledge that they need to execute a task by placing it on a "to do" list, but keep comfortably avoiding doing it by never assigning it a high enough priority to require immediate action.

Instead, they work on other activities that have a lower priority for success but feel more comfortable, like browsing the Internet instead of finishing the report for the boss.

Another common way to avoid noticing this mode of failure is to keep so busy that you tell yourself and others you are just "too busy" to get to it.

Penny was the queen of procrastination when faced with exercising according to her plans.

Escape Rituals

You cannot escape your way to success.

This evasion gimmick allows people to avoid the discomfort of taking needed actions by getting lost in some activity that they enjoy. Common examples of escape rituals are idle conversations, surfing the Web, playing computer games, fantasizing, watching TV programs, sleeping excessively, and reading for pleasure. These activities are not intrinsically bad. Actually, they may be a significant part of what a person does for enjoyment or relaxation.

The problem arises when people do these things *instead* of the activities needed to execute their success agenda.

Escaping Change-Discomfort to Pleasurable Activity

When you try to escape to a pleasurable activity when you have important but tedious or uncomfortable work to do, you encounter unintended consequences. We benefit when someone points out such follies to us because we rarely notice them on our own.

Pleasurable *Escapes* Don't Yield Needed Results

Penny was especially guilty of using a counterproductive escape ritual when facing an uncomfortable situation – she would simply escape into the pleasure of eating.

Simplistic Solutions

You cannot dodge your way to success.

This "seduction trap" mechanism enables people to satisfy their comfort priorities by taking apparently useful actions that do not actually effectively satisfy their success priorities.

This evasion mechanism creates three counterproductive "feelings benefits" at one time:

1. It overcomes the negative feelings associated with recognizing one is failing to improve.

2. Unlike with procrastination, rationalizations, or escape rituals, it substitutes a feeling that one is improving.

3. It avoids the discomfort of taking difficult actions to make the needed improvements.

An example might be if a person realized they were coming up short on their leadership abilities and frantically bought a book with a title such as *Become a Powerful Leader in 10 Easy Steps*. Buying the book may provide short-term emotional relief, but reading it will not overcome the deficiency that caused the distress in the first place. Becoming an excellent leader requires more effort than 10 easy steps.

We must pay our dues to make fundamental (auto-self) improvements and paying our dues means doing the necessary hard work to attain and sustain success. Simplistic solutions provide short-term feelings benefits that rob us of the focus and energy to make the needed changes to achieve long-term success.

Penny also used this gimmick many times. When she realized she had to change her diet and exercise more because she was not losing weight, she just purchased another diet book or program. Her action alleviated her discomfort of failure at losing weight and at the same time it made her feel that she was doing something beneficial to lose weight.

Excuses as Reasons

You cannot excuse your way to success.

People use this mechanism to avoid feeling bad about not completing a committed action. They attempt to fool themselves as well as others.

If you show up for work late and you explain that a wreck on the freeway shut traffic down and delayed you, that would be a *reason*. If, on the other hand, you show up late and say rush-hour traffic caused your delay, that would be an *excuse* to help you evade your responsibility to get to work on time. A responsible person would have left earlier to anticipate rush hour traffic and arrived at work on time.

Instead of taking responsibility for their own failures, people play the "blame game." They evade accountability by blaming somebody else or some situation for causing their failure.

Jake would often blame his employees for a particular failure in his own performance, and he would say they were not good enough for the position when they left for another job.

Discomfort Relentlessly Drives Us to
Evade the Arduous Habit-Change Path

I notice people using evasion gimmicks all the time. If my clients do it, I point it out to them. If others do it, politeness usually dictates that I simply watch them fail in their attempts to execute their success agenda.

Do you, anyone you work with, friends, or family ever use any of the above evasion gimmicks? What impact do you think these evasion gimmicks may have on achieving and maintaining successes for any of you?

Here is a summary of the five types of evasion gimmicks described in this chapter.

Insight:
Multiple Types of Evasion Gimmicks

Rationalization:	*Minimize importance:* Replace action with a story that action was not really needed.
Procrastination:	*Keep putting off:* Acknowledge task – keep it low priority – be "too busy."
Escape Rituals:	*Divert attention:* Do something pleasurable when faced with uncomfortable task.
Simplistic Solutions:	*Substitute:* Dodge needed action – take related action that does not achieve goal.
Excuses as Reasons:	*Pretend: Excuse* away lack of action by pretending you have a real *reason*.

6: The Unfair Fight

The unfair fight that concerns us here is the internal one that blocks us from accomplishing our goals and sustaining success.

The Auto-Self Normally Overpowers the Thinking-Self

An "unfair fight" occurs when the thinking-self tries to overpower the auto-self, such as by overcoming a compulsion or other bad habit by force of will. This "willpower" approach can work for short periods, but eventually tenacious comfort priorities, driven by the auto-self, grind down the success priorities created by the thinking-self. Because we unwittingly engage in and lose unfair fights so frequently, we recognize this unfair-fight as one of the fundamental principles of the two-selfs theory. New Year's resolutions normally do not work because they attempt to use intentions to overpower an auto-self characteristic. Transforming an auto-behavior or reconstructing an auto-context usually creates discomfort. I present many techniques later to avoid the unfair fight and effect needed changes.

Principle: **Unfair Fight**

This is a crucial concept. When our success and comfort priorities oppose each other, the normal reaction has the effect of trying to get the thinking-self to overpower the auto-self. This is an unfair fight because the auto-self is relentless and the discomfort it creates normally grinds down self-help efforts to establish lasting change.

Unfair fights occur in life. It happens when a big bully picks on a smaller kid. It happens whenever people go to Las Vegas to gamble; the casinos make sure the odds are stacked in their favor. It happens when someone plays the lottery; most people must lose so that a few players and the runners of the lottery can make a lot of money. If you pay attention to college football, it happens when Division 1A colleges play their annual early-season game against Division 1AA colleges; the former teams normally have bigger, faster, more-talented players, and about 20 more players on scholarship, creating an unfair fight that normally results in victory for the Division 1A teams.

Although all of the above activities create "unfair fights," that does not mean the underdog always loses. Occasionally smaller kids prevail over a bully, but fighting is still an activity that lightweights should avoid if possible.

Some people do win on a trip to Las Vegas, and, of course, someone eventually wins each lottery; however, prudent people will do well not to rely on these methods as a way to make a living. Division 1AA teams play against Division 1A teams for big financial payoffs, the opportunity to gain experience against superior players, and greater exposure. They occasionally win. The most famous case of winning this unfair fight was when Appalachian State beat #5-ranked Michigan in Ann Arbor on 9/1/07. However, any 1AA team hoping for an undefeated season would do well to avoid scheduling this inherently unfair fight.

The unfair fight that concerns us here is the internal one that blocks us from accomplishing our goals and sustaining success. It pits our intentions against our urges, driven by our auto-self, that compel and repel us – resulting in dueling dual priorities.

Penny encounters an unfair fight when she attempts to diet. Her thinking-self repeatedly creates an intention to manage her food intake. However, her auto-self relentlessly compels her to eat because that creates a source of pleasure that serves to mask whatever difficulty she is encountering in her life. Penny also encounters an unfair fight at work when she tries to avoid micromanaging all of the details of the assignments she gives to her subordinates. Even though she knows (a thinking-self activity) she needs to trust them and she sometimes gives them general directions and lets them figure out how to carry them out, she repeatedly falls back to managing all of the details (an unintentional auto-self driven activity). In addition, because Penny finds exercise boring and tedious, her auto-self blocks her ability to enact her thinking-self goal. These aspects of Penny illustrate well the pernicious way the unfair fight plays out. We sometimes succeed at individual attempts, which create hope for sustained success, but in the long run we almost always fail because auto-self-based feelings have greater lasting power than thinking-self-based intentions even when augmented with dogged willpower.

Interestingly, in our narrative so far about Jake, he has not engaged in an unfair fight. He has not created an explicit intention to change his behaviors, so he has not yet launched the effort to change himself that creates the internal reality wars that underpin the unfair fight. Jake is stuck at a different point; he is in denial. He cannot escape the auto-context change level that normally must precede an auto-behavior change. He has a deeply embedded self-image that runs counter to the feedback he has received from Lori, his bosses, and his coach. This creates an internal reality war because external information is impinging on an auto-self belief. If Jake manages to reconstruct his auto-context regarding his self-image, he will then encounter a struggle to change his auto-behaviors just as everybody else does.

Recognizing and learning to reconstruct obsolete or counterproductive auto-contexts can be as important to success as transforming a dysfunctional auto-behavior and the process is often equally difficult because both types of auto-self changes create discomfort.

Types of auto-context reconstructions that often play decisive roles in individual performance improvement and business success include dysfunctional attitudes, obsolete assumptions about the nature of the business and competition, and unrealistic self-images that block attempts to improve – as with Jake. I only mention this process here; I will focus a future book on the crucial role auto-contexts play on individual and organizational success. This book focuses on **auto-behaviors**.

With the help of his HR manager and a leadership performance survey, Mick, the CEO of the automotive supply company, was able to reconstruct his self-image and create an intention to moderate his behaviors. However, when Mick attempted to manage his abusive behavior, he was astonished to find out he could not control it. Mick came face-to-face with the debilitating unfair fight. He could not change his behavior even though he really wanted to do it to improve the performance of his company.

Behavioral transformations create unfair fights because the auto-self relentlessly induces discomfort that normally overpowers the success priority of transforming to a new desired behavior.

Recognizing the existence of this unfair fight and learning how to overcome it is a crucial breakthrough in our quest to maximize performance and to achieve sustained success.

Part II: A New Path to Change

Change your habits – change your destiny.

7:   Self-Help Is an Unfair Fight

*"Self-help programs inspire and create hope for a better future. Occasionally we succeed, but normally we fail because we cannot win the **unfair fight**."*

A fundamental difference between *self-help* and *guided-help* is that self-help programs create transient enthusiasm for change through powerful motivational events whereas guided-transformations create sustainable persistence and determination to improve through repeated motivational interventions.

How Does *Self-Help* Differ from *Learning*?

We cannot acquire new behaviors through study.

When we want to improve ourselves on our own by gaining more knowledge, we do not call it "self-help" (or "self-improvement"). We call it "reading," "listening," or "learning."

Exactly what is it then that we call "self-help?" To answer that question, we must utilize the insight that we operate in two modes. This enables us to see the difference between "self-help" and improvements through traditional "learning."

How Thinking-Self Improves

Self-improvement through information-based learning develops our thinking-self by acquiring greater knowledge from various information sources including books, journals, seminars, and the Internet.

We cannot acquire new behaviors through study. We improve our automatic activities through other means such as training, practice, experiential workshops, coaching, and self-help. Properly understood, therefore, self-help refers to changing our own auto-self; in particular, it normally refers to *transforming* an *auto-behavior* (an undesired habit) without external help except for "advice" on how to do it. So "**self-help**" really means "**self-transformation**."

> Definition: **Transformation**
>
> We call the process of changing an auto-behavior a "transformation." The goal of a habit-change coach or guide is to *transform* one or more undesired auto-behaviors of their clients.

One can receive guidance on self-help techniques for a wide variety of topics. The topic that concerns us here centers on improvements for attaining and sustaining success – in the work environment, where the organization defines success, and in personal lives, where we define what success means for ourselves.

In self-help efforts, people normally try to overcome a debilitating barrier to action, control a dysfunctional behavior, or develop a new positive behavior.

Most Self-Help Efforts Derail Due to the Unfair Fight

The enthusiasm created by self-help books and seminars normally lasts a few weeks at best.

Most self-help attempts fail because they rely on succeeding at the "unfair fight." That is, people attempt to use thinking-self intentions to overpower their tenacious auto-behaviors.

> Principle: **Self-Transformation is an Unfair Fight**
>
> Self-transformation, or attempting to transform an
> auto-behavior or auto-context through "self-help,"
> causes an unfair fight because the processes inherently
> create discomfort that we involuntarily take actions to
> avoid. This frequently results in termination of the
> transformation process before a permanent change is
> established. Our success priority, in the form of a
> thinking-self intention to change an auto-behavior,
> normally gets ground down by a comfort priority
> driven by our auto-self.

Our Intentions Cannot Overpower Our Auto-Self

Trying to eliminate deep-seated behaviors through self-help is like trying to stop a charging 800-pound gorilla with a peashooter. Both attempts may work as an economical first approach, but one should not count on them for survival or success. Would you try to make a living playing the lottery?

Self-help is the cheapest way to transform auto-behaviors. In cases where it works, you've won an unfair fight. In most cases, self-help fails. When the issue is crucial to your success, seek assistance from another person to serve as your guide.

The enthusiasm created by self-help books and seminars normally lasts a few weeks at best. To create lasting change can take a year or longer.

Because most transformations create discomfort, comfort priorities normally overwhelm the desire for change, leading to a poor success record for self-help behavior change.

As the enthusiasm and energy associated with self-help programs diminish, we involuntarily take actions to alleviate the discomfort associated with realizing we are failing to change an auto-self-driven habit despite our thinking-self intentions. The ubiquitous trick that many play on themselves is to use evasion gimmicks to avoid noticing they are failing in their attempt to create real, lasting change.

Now you understand why your New Year's resolutions fail so often and why so many people falter in their intentions to lead a healthier lifestyle.

The unfair fight is buried deep in human nature. Just as people do not always lose when they play a slot machine or bet on the lottery, people do not always lose unfair fights when trying to make personal improvements. However, none of these approaches provides a reliable path to sustained success.

Principle: **Transforming for Success**

Advanced societies provide education for success through universal education. We all learn, which means we create knowledge for our thinking-self in order to succeed. However, we now know that this is just one dimension of success. We also must have an auto-self profile that creates success through "doing" or executing consistently and not negatively affecting others through disruptive behaviors. The surest path to success is to complement our robust learning with periodic transforming to meet the needs of the environments we progressively encounter.

Overcoming Barriers to Action

"I know what I need to do, but I can't do it." – Morry

We All Have Barriers to Taking Some Needed Actions

Morry had a Ph.D., had been a full professor at a young age, and was widely published. When he came to me he was a high-level individual contributor in a top-end New York change management organization. He was extremely frustrated that he could not deal with aggressive people – especially ones in high authority.

Morry's inability to stay engaged when confronted with aggressive behavior was inconsistent with his desires and intentions to help CEOs of large companies. In his company, the most prestige and the highest income went to those who worked with CEOs.

Consistent feedback from performance reviews spanning several years had created in Morry a solid self-awareness about this issue. He tried repeatedly to overcome this crippling blockage on his own, but always to no avail. As he put it, "Something inside of me always forces me to retreat in the presence of powerful CEOs."

Morry's blockage was similar to Penny's inability to exercise regularly even though she was well aware of the consequences of not exercising.

As a guide, if you question clients (for simplicity, we will refer to people we help as "clients," even for unpaid guides) who want to overcome barriers at work, you will usually find that they have blockages to actions that cause them to fail in other aspects of their lives.

Penny's guide, Jeremy, probed and found out that besides her inability to exercise regularly or eat a healthy diet, she had an employee who would not meet commitments, and she was unable to hold him accountable.

When Morry and I explored other areas where he failed to take action, we identified two more.

His wife repeatedly got upset with him when his ex-wife dropped off their children at random times and without prior arrangement, which he allowed because he could not stand up to his ex-wife and insist that she agree to and abide by a drop-off schedule. He also created trouble for himself when he could not say "no" to speaking invitations and overbooked his time.

As we searched for a common behavioral cause for all of his issues, we concluded that he had a pattern of capitulating in the face of assertive people. Morry was used to figuring everything out but as he lamented to me, "I know what I need to do, but I can't do it."

Morry's coaching had a better ending than he had expected when he approached me. He went on to work effectively with CEOs and he also worked out an arrangement with his ex to reach agreement when Morry would have their children and he learned to accept only the most beneficial speaking engagements.

Morry and Penny experienced their own particular forms of action barriers. However, all of us fail to execute some items important to our success and well-being. Common examples in organizations are failure to conduct developmental performance reviews, inability to engage and resolve conflicts, avoidance of public speaking, failure to hold people accountable when they miss their commitments, and tenacious resistance to discovering our own uncontrollable actions – the problem that Jake has encountered.

The commonality in these examples and uncountable other ones is that, due to the unfair fight, self-help usually fails in trying to overcome significant action barriers.

Sidebar: **The Nature of Transformation**

Many people still believe that behavior transformations are impossible. They assert that important behavioral patterns are too deeply embedded in personality traits. "You can't teach an old dog new tricks." "A leopard never changes its spots." Many others do not understand why people do not change once they become aware of their counterproductive behaviors. They believe such people are lazy or just do not have the fortitude to make the change. The truth lies between these two extremes. We can transform most behaviors – even behaviors that appear to be personality traits. However, the process requires a keen understanding of our automatic mode, the application of techniques such as presented in this book, and systematic firm but empathetic support of a coach or guide.

Curtailing Behaviors That Harm Others

"I could not change my disruptive behaviors on my own no matter how hard I tried." – Mick

Disruptive Behaviors Are Counterproductive

Mick could not control his anger outbursts even after he became acutely aware of the negative effects they were having on his employees.

Earlier, I talked about my success at overcoming road rage through a self-help effort. Although excruciatingly difficult for me, that transformation was in a limited and easily noticed area. Self-help can work in some circumstances, but it is ineffective when faced with more-difficult challenges.

Jake struggled to accept his personal deficiencies. Once he overcomes that barrier, with considerable help, he will face another challenge of trying to curtail his counterproductive behaviors. Jake would have only a miniscule chance of changing his disruptive behaviors on his own.

Mick summed up the problem of changing his own disruptive behaviors: "Even after I recognized my abusive behavior, and even after I learned to notice it while I was doing it, I could not change my dysfunctional behaviors on my own no matter how hard I tried."

Most Self-Help Programs Are "Simplistic Solutions"

"Any port in a storm" usually does not work.

Simplistic solutions become "seduction traps" because we allow ourselves to *substitute* positive feelings for needed actions. We end up solving the wrong problem.

We use these simplistic solutions to alleviate the discomfort associated with realizing we are not where we want to be in life.

We may feel great when some new advice inspires us, but we end up not making the permanent changes that sustainable success requires.

This dilemma is particularly troublesome because the hopeful feelings make it seem so much like real benefits will surely come, but that is often not the case with the programs presented in self-help books, videos, and seminars.

These mechanisms often serve only to relieve our internal reality wars that emerge when we start to realize that some of our behaviors no longer match the requirements of our environment.

Unfortunately, ameliorating the discomfort of knowing that you need to change only blocks the initiatives, energy, and tenacity you need to mount a more-determined effort to make the transformations that actually benefit you. Some self-help programs offer comprehensive advice and exercises on how to stay with their program in spite of wanting to quit. However, many of these programs still end up being simplistic solutions instead of real paths to change.

Self-Help Normally Becomes a Seduction Trap

Many people succumb to the seduction trap in order to resolve their internal reality wars once they become aware of a conflict between an auto–behavior (habit) or auto-context (paradigm, thought pattern, mindset) and feedback from the environment. Instead of engaging in heavy lifting to change an undesired habit, they inadvertently take what feels like an easy way out by employing a simplistic solution.

Penny fell back into a seduction trap every time she wanted to regain her former figure and tried another "weight loss made easy" program.

The imperative to satisfy our comfort needs is so powerful that often people unintentionally seek to escape change at the expense of their success.

"Any port in a storm" usually doesn't work because, like Homeric sirens sweetly beckoning sailors to their demise, many of the improvement ports are seductive lairs of entrapment that lead to failure.

To succeed at habit change, observe this formula:

- Behavior change causes discomfort.
- We involuntarily take action to avoid discomfort.
- Therefore, arrange for a guide or coach to help you through the discomfort of transformational change.

Self-Help Programs Are Better at Inspiring Than Transforming

Transient enthusiasm does not equal transformational change.

Because so many people desire to find ways to improve their chances of success, there is an eager market for inexpensive and seemingly easy self-help programs. As such, self-help offerings run the gamut from dubious approaches sold by charlatans to well thought-out, experience-tempered approaches that often do help people improve themselves on some issues.

The book, *50 Self-Help Classics: 50 Inspirational Books to Transform Your Life, From Timeless Sages to Contemporary Gurus,* by Tom Butler-Bowdon provides a summary of 50 historical and present-day approaches to self-help.

That book provides an excellent vehicle to survey the landscape of self-improvement. It includes a wide assortment of approaches ranging from practical to mystical. Since all of these books contain at least nuggets of good advice on how to improve one's self, positive changes sometimes occur.

However, a common thread is that they provide plausible advice but fall short on effective techniques. Since most of the reviewed books have sold well, it follows that another attribute of these books is that they inspire.

Inspirational self-help programs can provide motivation and energy to attempt to make significant changes, but they frequently fail to turn that motivation into transformation. Transient enthusiasm does not equal transformational change.

A good way to receive sustained motivation to make transformational change is to engage a trusted guide.

8. The Transformation Guide

A transformation guide can fill the gap between self-help and professional habit-change coaching.

Self-help efforts require only a small financial investment and normally provide little external support; unfortunately, discomfort associated with transformational change derails most attempts at self-change.

Professional transformation coaches achieve extremely reliable results, but the investment exceeds what most individuals and smaller companies are willing or able to make.

A transformation guide, often in the form of a friend or colleague, can fill the gap between self-help and professional habit-change coaching.

Trusted Transformation Guide

This book focuses on overcoming the *inherent* unreliability of self-help attempts by obtaining help from a transformation guide. This book also provides techniques that can enable you to guide a friend or colleague through transformational change.

Three Approaches to Transforming an Auto-Behavior

Here is a summary of three approaches to transform a counterproductive auto-behavior:

1. Enroll in a self-help program/seminar or buy a book or a set of DVDs. Self-help programs are like playing the lottery – sometimes they succeed, but most of the time they fail. Because of the debilitating effects of the unfair fight and of evasion gimmicks that keep us from escaping it, I estimate that the success rate over the huge spectrum of self-help efforts is less than 10%.

2. Use this book to recruit and train a trusted transformation guide who can help you through the behavior-change process. Guided change is intrinsically more successful than self-help programs because it addresses the debilitating effects of the unfair fight. In addition, a good guide will expose your evasive gimmicks, keep you on track with your goals, and repeatedly support you in your effort to meet your behavior-change intentions. Because trusted transformation guides will provide ongoing support and can make use of any available self-help process, in addition to the transformation techniques described in this book, I estimate that they should succeed in the 25% to 40% range. That could

quadruple your chances of success compared with attempting to change an undesired habit using your own self-help efforts.

3. Retain a professional transformation coach who will work with you until you succeed. Make sure any transformation coach you select:

- Understands the automatic mode of human activities in considerable depth

- Has the ability to withstand assertive pushback and continue to nudge you empathetically but firmly through the discomfort of change

- Has mastered a large repertoire of proven techniques

Master Coaches will succeed upwards of 90% of the time; the major exceptions being people who were forced into the coaching process rather than those who embraced it. Transformation coaches help their clients change when the clients want to but cannot do it on their own. Once a coach determines that a client does not want to change, it is best to terminate the engagement. In our ongoing narrative of Jake, we had reached the point of terminating his coaching program if he did not soon recognize his counterproductive auto-self issues. Because this method requires significant time from an expert coach, it usually entails a corresponding investment by the client.

Comparing Three Approaches to Habit Change

(Author's estimates)

	Option 1	Option 2	Option 3
Approach	Self-Help	Trusted Guide	Master Coach
Success Rate	<10%	~25%-40%	>90%
Improvement	base	~4x self-help	>10x self-help
Investment	<$500	Quid pro quo	$20K-$50K

Definition: **Transformation Guide**

A *transformation guide* is a friend, colleague, or family member who, through repeated support and the use of habit-change techniques such as found in this book, can help someone transform an auto-behavior. A guided transformation effort is inherently more effective than self-help because it can use all of the self-help techniques plus provide ongoing support and expose evasion gimmicks to help the client overcome the unfair fight. A *professional coach* differs from a *trusted guide* in having deeper experience, more techniques, and normally a greater ability to withstand the discomfort from pushback associated with the inevitable resistance to change.

Jeremy picked up enough techniques during his engagement with an expert coach that he could now effectively guide friends to transform many of their counterproductive behaviors, as he was about to start with Penny.

Jerry, the head of quality assurance for an engine manufacturing company, changed so much in ways he had not imagined that he went on to leverage his experience by guiding some of his team members. He guided them to overcome similar barriers to those he had suffered when attempting to attain consistent results from people outside of their organization.

Bruce, the CFO of the industrial manufacturing company, became so concerned about the gaps he had in effectively leading his organization that he decided to take action on his own. He put it this way, "When I realized I did not understand the significant impact my automatic activities have on my performance and the success of my organization, I decided to transfer some of what I learned and experienced through the coaching process to my team. I contracted to have leadership surveys performed on my direct reports and, as I expected, many auto-self issues emerged for all of them, and they were mostly unaware of their counterproductive auto-behaviors. After I got them to recognize and accept their behaviors that were undermining our further success, I decided to coach them on my own because our budget would not accommodate an external coach this year. I am pleased, and so are they, that I was able to help some of them change undesired behaviors, which resulted in improving their performance."

Bruce became a transformation guide.

Characteristics of a Good Transformation Guide

Characteristics to look for in transformation guides:

- They do not just read, but also study the techniques in this book.

- They are committed to helping you transform for **your** reasons, not theirs.

- They are willing to guide you until you complete your transformation – several months.

- They have some ability to withstand your inevitable pushback while guiding you through your behavior change.

- They are not associated with the behavioral issues you want changed.

Guides need to nudge their clients through the distress they experience during the habit-change process. The guide will also experience discomfort when clients inevitably push back (as, for instance, when the guide exposes an explanation as an *excuse* rather than a *reason*). This can hinder unprepared guides in adequately escorting clients through their change discomfort.

When training new coaches, I often need to coach them through this blockage to action. Since most guides won't have the luxury of receiving this type of training, it is essential to select a guide who can manage his or her own feelings and display empathy while pushing and pulling those they guide through the transformation process. Accordingly, it is best to avoid selecting a person as a guide who fails to give candid performance reviews, doesn't hold people accountable when they miss a commitment, recoils in the presence of aggressive people, or habitually retreats when encountering conflict.

A Guide's Commitment

To establish a permanent change in a habit takes quite a while – as much as a year. The process can deceive us because we often get results right away. However, if we terminate the coaching process too early, the client usually will revert to the old habit. My experience is that one year is a reliable time to make the new auto-behavior permanent.

The process also can involve some bumps as the guide leads the client through the discomfort of, and concomitant resistance to, change. A transformation guide must commit to the necessary investment of time and tenacity in the face of such friction.

(Cautionary note: Avoid exceeding the bounds of pragmatic help. If your client reveals a chemical dependency, refer her or him to a drug rehab program. If your client appears to suffer from a serious psychiatric problem, refer him or her to a mental-health professional.)

My normal coaching engagement consists of two one-hour sessions per week. But, I usually coach on multiple issues. If you agree to guide change for someone or if you recruit a transformation guide for yourself, the engagement will likely focus on a single issue. Two short sessions (10-

15 minutes) per week will work better than one longer session because of more frequent support. The good news is that we can conduct most sessions on the phone, so that minimizes disruptions. I normally start a coaching engagement with a face-to-face session and then conduct one face-to-face session per month – even for remote clients. For someone you know well, you can skip the face-to-face or substitute a video session. The most important factors for success are frequency of sessions and duration of the engagement.

Insight: **Reciprocal Coaching/Guidance**

When you want to have somebody guide you through transforming an undesired auto-behavior, you may get lucky and know a person who will spend two sessions a week for up to a year without expecting something back, but more often you will need to provide some consideration in return. An appropriate quid pro quo would be to offer to guide your helper through a transformation. That would establish the simplest form of reciprocal, or peer, transformation guidance. You will each do a better job of helping the other when you experience the process yourself. I always insist that people I train to coach experience the process themselves from the client side so they understand what it feels like to their clients. An even better approach is to enlist two or more colleagues to perform round-robin peer coaching. This approach has two distinct advantages. Each pairing has a fixed guide/client relationship and avoids having to change roles repeatedly with each other. Also, if one participant drops out, the chain can get re-linked so that nobody gets dropped in the middle of their transformation process.

9. Providing Repeated Support

Repeated support, in the form of hope and encouragement, helps to overcome the unfair fight.

Self-help often fails because it is inherently an unfair fight. The deck is always stacked against changing habitual behaviors because deep change innately creates discomfort, and we involuntarily avoid such suffering.

Principle: Repeated Support

Repeated support is the antithesis of self-help and it can overcome the process that renders self-help so unreliable – succumbing to the unfair fight. The support works through repeatedly providing hope and encouragement and empathetically yet firmly nudging clients through the discomfort of transformational change. Self-help programs often provide intense, but transient motivation. Repeated support provides sustained motivation.

By repeatedly applying support, we can help people improve their chances of success by re-establishing hope and nudging them through the uncomfortable aspects of behavior transformation.

Valuable characteristics that a transformation guide should have in order to provide the needed support are empathy for the discomfort of change, interpersonal skills to help clients through their reflexive resistance to change, and the internal fortitude to withstand the inevitable pushback when escorting someone through the habit-change process.

Having regular support greatly improves the chances of succeeding at transformational change.

Transformation Guide Providing Support

As the image illustrates, the repeated support provided by a transformation guide can prevent the client from sliding down the slippery slope of faltering resolve, then backsliding, and eventually terminating the change effort due to the persistent discomfort of the change process.

Technique:
Providing Repeated Support

What This Technique Means:
Repeated support is the antidote to the unfair fight people encounter when they try to transform an auto-behavior on their own.

How to Use This Technique:
Pull your clients by inducing pleasure in the form of hope, focus on incremental gains toward their grand goals, and celebrating each time they enact an intention. *Push* your clients with discomfort whenever they fail to enact an intention to change. To maximize the value of the support, plan to have at least brief sessions twice a week.

Why This Technique Works:
The repeated support works by *counteracting* the discomfort inherent in transformational behavior change. It keeps the client moving forward by providing *destination motivation* (pleasure in incremental victories when moving toward grand goals – the purpose of trying to change) and *progress motivation* (celebrations of enacting new behaviors and laments at failing to enact intended behaviors).

Penny Gets Support

Penny agreed to meet with Jeremy, her best friend Kristen's new boyfriend, on a Saturday afternoon to discuss this new concept about the two selfs that would help Penny lose and keep off the 50 pounds of extra weight. The three of them met at Penny's house at 1:00 pm.

"I know you work at the Post Office, but I really don't know what you do there," Jeremy began with Penny.

"I'm the team supervisor for international mail. What's this have to do with me losing weight?" she replied timidly

"You'll see," Jeremy said. "Now how many people do you supervise?"

"I lead three others, and we make sure mail going to different countries is routed to the correct airlines."

Digging deeper, Jeremy asked, "Do you get along with everyone on your team?"

Penny frowned. "Why do you need to know that?"

Jeremy watched her closely.

"Do I need to tell him this?" Penny asked Kristen.

"You need to trust him," Kristen offered, calming her friend's resistance. "I know that may be hard for you right now, but believe me, what he does worked for me and it can work for you."

Penny looked very uncomfortable.

"Listen, Penny," Kristen went on. "You are a very attractive woman with a very pretty face, but you could be more attractive – a knockout – if you lost that extra weight. You and I both know this."

"I've tried everything to lose weight," Penny said, becoming emotional. "I attended seminars and I would leave absolutely positive that I was going to lose weight in the next month by steadfastly following what they said. The first week it was great and then as the weeks wore on and nothing seemed to happen I eventually lost my enthusiasm and went back to my old eating habits."

"That's because change is uncomfortable," Jeremy began to explain. "When I worked with my transformation coach, the hardest thing for me was to control my anger outbursts – especially when I had a bad day or we didn't finish a project on time. It was extremely uncomfortable for me. I had to learn to counteract those painful feelings by telling myself that my outbursts were holding me back and bad for my career."

Penny took a deep breath; her whole body seemed to heave. Jeremy's observations and questions were touching sensitive areas for Penny – ones he strongly suspected were integral to her obstacles to losing weight.

Penny decided to follow Kristen's advice and give Jeremy the benefit of the doubt, saying, "All right. If you really want to know, I don't get along with everybody at work. This one guy on my team is a real jerk. Always pushing the envelope to do things his way; always in my face. The two women are OK, but I feel I'm doing most of the work while they just take up space."

"And what does your boss say about this?" Jeremy inquired further.

"I haven't got around to telling him yet," Penny admitted.

Jeremy put his hand on his chin and his eyes became distant.

"And your husband? What was he like?"

"Former husband!" Penny said with a clear note of indignity.

"A lot like this guy at work – a jerk. Always putting me down, getting into my face, telling me what to do."

"And what did you do?" Jeremy asked, gently pressing further.

"Not much," she confided. "He was a lot bigger and louder than me. I always wanted to shout back at him, tell him off, but I never got the chance."

Jeremy now thought he had enough information to offer a tentative observation about Penny's auto-self issues. "Here are my initial impressions. You either procrastinate or eat when faced with a hard decision. You struggle to deal effectively with aggressive people and you are afraid to hurt the feelings of your team by pointing out their inadequacies, so they use you and don't do their share of the work."

"You can't effectively lead people and you can't manage your weight. Your auto-behavior causes both issues. You do them habitually and unknowingly."

Penny put her head down and Kristen got up and sat next to her.

"This is the hard part, Penny – finding out the cause of your problems and then accepting it."

"If you feel this is the cause of your problems, then we can work to 'reprogram' your habits to make sure they're not working against your desires," Jeremy added.

Penny looked up at Jeremy, her eyes rimmed in red.

"I'm not upset at what you said. I'm upset because I'm starting to see the real problem that you pointed out – my avoidance of tough stuff. This feels real to me, and now I'm starting to see how I sabotage my life."

"This is the first step in the right direction – recognizing your barriers to action," Jeremy said.

Penny was contemplative, staring at the ceiling and thinking back to situations in her past.

Then she said quietly, "This is like someone turned on a light. I can go back to many situations and see where I could have acted differently. It always seemed like something inside of me kept me from doing what I really wanted to do." She looked at Jeremy and said, "I wish I knew this earlier."

Jeremy alerted Penny to the difficulties associated with auto-behavior change. "Penny, understanding the scope of your undesired behaviors and getting an idea of what underlying issues may cause them is a good start. However, your real challenge lies ahead of you as you know from your attempts to lose weight. Changing habits is so difficult because it creates discomfort, which causes most people to quit. I commit to you that as long as you keep working on your habit changes I will stay with you for a whole year and provide repeated support to help you work your way through your changes."

"I can't believe you would do that for me," Penny exclaimed. "I have repeatedly failed to change on my own. I am really looking forward to trying this with your help. How can I ever repay you?"

Jeremy chuckled. "You're Kristen's best friend, so now you're my friend too, and this will get me lots of points with Kristen. Besides, I really enjoy helping people who have tried but failed to change on their own."

Types of Coaches

Because there are no licensing requirements for coaches, many people call themselves "coaches" while providing vastly different levels of help.

At the high end of the coaching profession are two distinct types of coaches: advisory coaches and transformation coaches.

Advisory coaches, also known as consultants, provide specialized and timely information to business executives. Many people providing these services are very bright and deeply experienced, and add high value.

When an executive has difficulty implementing some of the sound advice, advisory coaches may attempt to change interfering behaviors, but that is normally not their area of expertise, so behavior change attempts often come up short. Advisory coaches provide most of their value to the *thinking-self* of executives.

Transformation coaches focus on changing counterproductive behaviors of executives and other leaders in organizations. They specialize in transforming aspects of their clients' *auto-behaviors* that block their performance or create disruptions in the organization. The few transformation coaches who have executive experience also add value by providing guidance on management and leadership issues, but that is not their main focus.

It can help to look at this distinction from different perspectives:

Advisory Coaching/Guiding	**Transformational Coaching/Guiding**
Helps people *manage* better.	Helps people *lead* better.
Helps people *know more* quickly.	Helps people *behave* better and *execute* better.

Anybody wanting to help someone change an undesired habit, including those who call themselves "life coaches," professional/executive transformation coaches, and transformation guides can add value by providing a supportive environment that self-help programs inherently lack. Adding powerful techniques, as described in the following chapters, based on an understanding of the automatic mode of human activities, can create solid results in addition to the general support.

Part III: Techniques for Change

*Transforming gets people to do what they
previously failed to do repeatedly, and
to stop doing what they used to do compulsively.
It "rewires" their comfort priorities.*

10: The Counteracting Principle

Fight fire with fire. Use induced feelings to counteract innate feelings that drive undesired automatic behaviors.

Overcoming the Unfair Fight

"How can I make the fight 'fair' or tilt it in my favor so I can change?" – Penny

Even when we recognize the need to change an undesired habit, we rarely succeed on our own due to the *unfair fight*.

This transformation "fight" is "unfair" because relentless, counterproductive comfort priorities normally wear down our thinking-self intentions. These comfort priorities keep us from success because we often feel like staying in a known, comfortable place more than we want to change. We reflexively use evasion gimmicks including procrastination, escape rituals, simplistic solutions, rationalization, and excuses to avoid feeling bad about failing to achieve our goals.

These evasion gimmicks allow us to avoid the immediate discomfort associated with acting contrary to our comfort priorities. They also simultaneously rob us of the drive to execute effectively or to transform undesired habits.

We have seen that one antidote to the venom of the
unfair fight is to use external resources to help guide us
through the discomfort of completing disliked tasks or
transforming our unwanted habits.

External help works most effectively if the helper
understands some effective techniques for getting us to
execute our success priorities (our plans) when our comfort
priorities (our feelings) work against us. Two effective
methods that can overcome comfort priorities to achieve a
transformation are

- **Counteracting** the auto-self-based feelings that drive
  bad habits and block transformational change
- **Recontextualizing** the auto-contexts (attitudes,
  expectations) that frame how we relate to people and
  situations

The Counteracting Principle

The thinking-self initiates transformational change but
usually cannot win the battle against the auto-self due
to the unfair fight. A clever way around this losing
battle is to induce feelings that counteract the feelings
and drives that perpetuate the unwanted behavior. For
habit change, this is the central principle of the two-
selfs theory because it underpins many of the
transformation techniques.

When Penny learned about the unfair fight from Jeremy,
it made her feel a little better. She exclaimed, "At least now
I don't feel like such a pathetic wimp for not getting control

of my weight." Then she asked Jeremy, "How can I make the fight 'fair' or tilt it in my favor so I can change?"

Jeremy replied, "I can help you overcome the unfair fight by repeatedly giving you encouragement and support so that you don't falter. I also think I know enough about how to use techniques to counteract the discomfort that blocks your transformation that I can guide you to establish healthy habits that will enable you to lose the weight and keep it off permanently."

I have encountered coaches who assert they do not believe in inducing discomfort in their clients because it goes against their ethics. Transforming habitual behaviors requires overcoming auto-self comfort drives that create resistance to change, and the best way to do that is by inducing positive and negative *counteracting* feelings.

There is nothing unethical about inducing discomfort to guide people to achieve their improvement goals. It is no different than giving candid feedback during performance reviews. In fact, coaches and guides must induce feelings to help their clients overcome habit-change discomfort that blocks most self-help attempts because of the unfair fight.

No matter how many times you explain it to them (a thinking-self activity), clients inevitably push back when they experience the discomfort (an auto-self activity) of avoiding the old undesired behavior. This pushback often becomes quite assertive and therefore creates discomfort in the coach/guide that they must accept while continuing the transformation process. If the transformation coach relents and allows some regression to past behavior, that would ultimately derail the change effort.

Sidebar: *Descriptive Stage* of Development

Until a few decades ago, we were in the *ignorance stage* regarding our automatic mode's role in success and performance improvements. More recently, we have been in the *metaphoric stage* ("soft," "people process," "elephant," "box"). Metaphors inform us that something important is out there, but they do not allow us to manage the newly discovered items very well. Metaphors shine a light in a new direction. Detailed descriptions enable us to understand what we now see. We have now entered the *descriptive stage* where we can describe the automatic mode in sufficient detail to understand it explicitly and manage it systematically. The **principles** and **properties** in this book provide empowering descriptions of our two selfs.

	Metaphoric Stage	Descriptive Stage
Behaviors/ execution	Getting outside the "box"	Transform an **auto-behavior**
Thought patterns	Thinking outside the "box"	Transform an **auto-context**

Sidebar: **New Terminology**

In the **metaphoric stage**, we use existing terminology and create new meanings via associations with current meanings. In the **descriptive stage**, we must either define new explicit meanings for existing words or create some new terminology. Thus, we say we have two "selfs" to refer to our two mental modes. We also use the form "auto-" to remind ourselves of the activities that work automatically, independent of intentions and to call attention to the similarity among seemingly unrelated items (auto-self, auto-behaviors, auto-contexts, auto-skills, and auto-expertise). To minimize complexity, we have kept the new terminology to a minimum and have identified it in the Definitions and Principles boxes.

11: Don't Attack, Counteract

You cannot study or think your way through habit change; you must _feel_ your way through it.

After most people recognize that some of their automatic behaviors have repeatedly contributed to their underachievement or failure, they become strong-willed and determined to stop that behavior in order to achieve and maintain success. But, using intentions and willpower to attack impeding comfort priorities rarely works – as illustrated in the earlier descriptions of the unfair fight and Penny's repeated failure to lose weight through self-help techniques.

Once people recognize their undesired behaviors, the challenge is not figuring out how to overpower those errant behaviors, but rather to find a way to induce feelings that *counteract* the auto-self feelings that drive the unwanted behaviors. This overcomes the unfair fight and levels the playing field.

Fortunately, we can induce feelings in the auto-self that *counteract* the ingrained feelings (fight fire with fire) instead of trying to overpower the auto-self with strong intentions and tenacious willpower. However, individuals usually cannot induce counteracting feelings on their own and must use a trusted person as a transformation guide or hire a professional transformation coach to reach their goals.

Techniques for Counteracting Undesirable Behaviors

Induce feelings that counteract ingrained auto-self feelings that perpetuate an undesired behavior.

Counteract Rather Than Try to Overpower the Auto-Self

Our thinking-self needs to act like a judo black belt to counter the superior power of our auto-self. To do that we must induce feelings that counteract ingrained auto-self feelings that perpetuate an undesired behavior or create a barrier to action.

To counteract the discomfort that blocks a step in the transformation process, one must induce either positive or negative feelings. Two ways to do that are:

1. Create a *path of least discomfort*. **Make it more uncomfortable to avoid the action than to take it**. This process *pushes* people through the feelings that have blocked their success.

2. Induce pleasure in taking an action that overpowers the discomfort of taking it. This process *pulls* people through their uncomfortable feelings that have blocked their success actions.

It normally works best to both push and pull clients through the transformation process.

The path of least discomfort may seem like a technique we should avoid. If the needed action already creates discomfort, why in the world would we want to induce still greater discomfort? Because it gets results! It enables us to execute our success agenda, which ultimately is much more rewarding than avoiding the short-term discomfort that is required to achieve lasting change.

Using the pull of pleasure to overcome the discomfort of doing a difficult task seems like a more humane approach. Can we simultaneously experience pleasure and feel discomfort about the same task? Yes, we can. Think about the joy of accomplishing a difficult task. It was uncomfortable while you did the task, but the anticipation of accomplishing that task was pleasurable.

In addition to helping people get past their barriers to action, coaches and guides can also employ similar push (discomfort) and pull (pleasure) techniques to counteract the internal (auto-self driven) pleasure or drive that causes us to display disruptive behaviors or to take other actions that undermine our success.

The key to the counteracting principle is to *induce* feelings that counteract *ingrained* auto-self feelings that perpetuate an undesired behavior.

The Path of Least Discomfort

"Ouch!"

The path of least discomfort does not sound appealing, but others have used it on you throughout your life and I suspect you use it on other people now.

Before reading on, try to figure out when you have experienced getting results through the path of least discomfort.

Once we identify a common use of this general technique, we can begin to use this process more broadly.

Have you figured the common usage of the path of least discomfort? ...

It's deadlines. And deadlines work because they create a path of least discomfort.

You encounter this at work or school when a project is due. Most homework assignments are not fun, and many business projects are not a joy either. In both cases, discomfort often causes us to put the task off – to procrastinate. As the deadline approaches, our discomfort rises. We no longer just *think* about possible consequences, we start to *feel* them.

At school, we would receive a lower grade if we did not turn the assignment in on time. As the deadline approached, our anxiety increased regarding potential bad grades, a lower GPA, and other consequences.

At work, we experience an escalating set of potential penalties as a deadline approaches. "If I don't finish this assignment on time, my boss may chew me out, or worse yet, I may get a poor rating on my next review. It could get even worse; I may not get a bonus, and I may receive a low raise next year. Oh no, I may not get the promotion I'm expecting."

As the deadline becomes imminent, panic sets in. "If I don't get this project done on time, they may demote me. I can't stand it; what if they fire me because I miss this important deadline?"

As the deadline approaches ever nearer, the discomfort of not doing the task eventually becomes greater than the discomfort associated with doing the task, and we get it done. Whew, just in time!

Now you know the underlying reasons why deadlines work so effectively. Deadlines are an excellent example of an *empirically-derived* (that is, through experience rather than based on a theory) process that normally produces the desired result. As we embrace the two-selfs theory, deadlines provide a common example of the path of least discomfort to attain results. The path of least discomfort is one form of the *theoretically-derived* counteracting principle. Using a theory enables us to create additional techniques and have high confidence they will work. All of the techniques presented in this book worked "out of the box" (i.e., the first time and repeatedly) as expected.

Technique:
Constructing a Path of Least Discomfort

What This Technique Means:
The path of least discomfort creates needed action by making it more uncomfortable to avoid the action than to do it.

How to Use This Technique:
Notice and politely but firmly point out to clients when they fail to do what they claim they want to do for their success.

Why This Technique Works:
The path of least discomfort is the most common use of the counteracting principle to get something accomplished. This mechanism underpins other techniques such as exposing the use of evasion gimmicks or a failure to enact a declared intention; it also makes deadlines effective.

Because we use it so frequently in coaching (and in holding people accountable for meeting commitments), we give a name ("the path of least discomfort") to the technique of instilling greater discomfort to get a client to accomplish an uncomfortable activity. However, transformation guides should also recognize and use the other three forms of counteraction techniques:

1. Push people past barriers to action through inducing pleasure that counteracts the discomfort blocking the action. For example, we repeatedly induced pleasurable feelings associated with regaining her previous figure to get Penny to go workout at her gym.
2. Use pleasurable feelings to counteract the auto-self pleasure or drive that causes counterproductive behaviors. For example, we used the pleasure of becoming more attractive to counteract the pleasure and comfort Penny got out of eating.
3. Instill discomfort to counteract the auto-self pleasure or drive that causes undesired behaviors. We employed this form of counteraction with Penny by having her go look in the mirror every time she reached for a treat she had decided she wanted to avoid.

The path of least discomfort plays such a big role in transformational coaching because we normally apply it first to break the old habit or barrier. We then apply pleasure to reinforce the new, substitute behavior. If we look a little deeper into the transformation process, we can see that even when it appears that we are inducing discomfort to overcome the pleasure derived from a bad habit (such as indulgent eating, smoking, displaying anger, intimidating), we are really employing the path of least discomfort because it is so uncomfortable to break the habit. We provide a dramatic example of coaching Don to break his smoking habit in Chapter 15: Applying Virtual Conditioning.

Sidebar: **Theory-Based Improvements**

In the *metaphoric stage* of development, **empirical techniques** emerge, some of which can produce good results. Practitioners create empirical techniques by trial and error and testing for effectiveness often without understanding how they work. The use of deadlines is an example of an empirically derived technique that works effectively.

The *descriptive stage* enables us to create **theory-based techniques** that provide dependable, repeatable processes for change. The transformation techniques in this book are built upon a solid theory of our two selfs. You will see in Chapter 14: Declaring Anchors for Change, that when we understand deadlines as one example of an overarching technique of using the path of least discomfort, we can extend the general technique into areas other than deadlines.

How to Induce Counteracting Feelings

More-powerful techniques also exist.

Transformation guides or coaches can employ two opposite counteracting techniques simultaneously. They can *push* people, as with a deadline, by inducing discomfort if their clients fail to complete the desired action and they can *pull* them by inducing pleasure in the anticipation of, and progress toward, successfully executing unintended behavior.

This looks promising, but how does one go about inducing targeted feelings? The most common way is the threat or implied threat of real punishments if that person fails to take a critical action or displays an undesired behavior. However, more sophisticated and ultimately more powerful techniques also exist.

We have already described two specific counteracting techniques:

- Providing Repeated Support
- Constructing a Path of Least Discomfort

Here are three new powerful techniques for inducing counteracting feelings:

- **Instilling virtual consequences**
- **Exposing evasion gimmicks**
- **Posing evocative open questions**

The following chapters describe, give examples, and explain the usage of these and other techniques. However, before we can apply transformation techniques, we must recognize our undesirable auto-behaviors. We do not normally recognize that we have auto-behaviors that undermine our effectiveness because they usually take place outside of our awareness and independent of our intentions. And, most people avoid taking actions to learn about their auto-behaviors because they would rather remain blissfully complacent with their current self-image. Therefore, the first step in transforming to a fundamentally new level of performance is to recognize the strengths and limitations of our auto-behaviors.

12: Recognizing Precedes Transforming

"Mirror, mirror on the wall ..."

Who are you and who do you want to be?

Are you a *doer* who consistently executes important actions and a *leader* who persistently motivates and develops others?

How confident are you that you understand your strengths and limitations, especially those elusive automatic actions and behaviors, which none of us fully recognize until we receive and accept feedback from multiple sources?

How likely is it that you will reach your full potential if you do not gain empowering self-awareness and then take actions to leverage your strengths and overcome your weaknesses?

To improve our automatic activities, we must first gain visibility into our success-producing characteristics – the profile of our strengths and weaknesses.

Self-Awareness about What?

"The most effective leaders are self-aware, while a lack of self-awareness is strongly related to derailment." – Center for Creative Leadership

One has to establish penetrating self-awareness to achieve performance improvements. Richard Ketterer and Michael Chayes discuss this need in *Discontinuous Change: Leading Organizational Transformation* by David A. Nadler, et al.

"Increased self-awareness…is especially critical for senior managers…The more insight managers gain about themselves, the better able they are to act consistently with their intentions."

The Center for Creative Leadership's *Handbook of Leadership Development* asserts, "The most effective leaders are self-aware, while a lack of self-awareness is strongly related to derailment."

Jake's career was about to derail unless we could drive him through his blockage to action to accept his behavioral deficiencies. His self-awareness was deficient in a debilitating way.

The *Handbook of Leadership Development* goes on to state, "Our research and experience, as well as the research done by others, show that self-awareness is a key attribute of effective leaders."

We are already aware of what we say and the actions we deliberately perform. So, what exactly is it that we are unaware of that blocks our improvements?

The two-selfs theory of human activities enables us to add teeth to these assertions about the need for empowering self-awareness. We need not concern ourselves about awareness of our thinking-self's activities. We unavoidably recognize our thoughts and our explicit knowledge (even though we may sometimes fail to notice when our thought stream jumps from topic to topic). Our strategies, plans, and task lists inherently require focused awareness. In fact, the single thought-stream of our thinking-self consumes nearly all of the bandwidth of our awareness, which usually keeps us from noticing our auto-self's activities.

When performance improvement or leadership researchers argue for increasing self-awareness as a forerunner to improving performance, they really mean awareness of our auto-self's automatic behaviors, thought patterns (auto-contexts – paradigms, cultural artifacts), and leadership skills.

We already discussed two properties of the auto-self:

1. Auto-self activities take place outside of our normal awareness.
2. Auto-self activities happen independently from our intentions.

Therefore, if we do not receive and embrace feedback from helpful external resources, we normally remain trapped in a distorted view of our automatic activities.

If we do not have a realistic understanding of our auto-self characteristics, we cannot recognize when our uncontrollable activities no longer match the needs of our organization, our position in it, or our personal environment. Deteriorating results often follow. We also may fail to recognize our own auto-self strengths, and therefore we do not leverage them for maximum effectiveness.

"We call this recognizing type of awareness "*static* self-awareness" because it is a one-time event for any given auto-self characteristic such as frequently displaying anger or regularly procrastinating when it is time to exercise as with Jake and Penny, respectively.

Principle: *Static* Self-Awareness

Static self-awareness occurs when you *recognize* that you have a certain auto-self characteristic. This is not easy because our auto-self activities normally take place outside of our awareness, so we do not notice our auto-behaviors and therefore do not recognize our auto-behaviors' characteristics until someone imposes awareness on us. Discomfort inherent in the discovery process further impedes achieving static self-awareness of our auto-self characteristics.

The Agony of Self-Discovery

Most people prefer self-deception to self-discovery.

Improving the auto-self provides the greatest leverage for sustaining success because our automatic activities have eluded the deep understanding that leads to systematic improvement.

However, an enormous barrier to sustaining success comes from involuntary resistance to discovering one's own auto-self characteristics, which must precede a cooperative auto-self-improvement program. We must recognize our own auto-self characteristics before we can get help in overcoming them.

You May Not Be the Star You Believe You Are

"Mirror, mirror on the wall..." People maintain a self-image that resides at least partly in auto-contexts. Sometimes auto-self images of one's abilities and value do not align with the realities observed by others or demonstrated by actual performance.

When self-images underrate actual or potential performance, people tend to underachieve. They fail to take needed actions because they lack self-confidence.

For high-level managers, the opposite often prevails. Past successes may have constructed a grandiose self-image that masks severe flaws, as was the case with Jake. This hides the reality that successes may have come *in spite of*, rather than *because of*, some personal characteristics.

Either way, people often have inaccurate self-concepts, which interfere with their ability to maximize their effectiveness and satisfaction in business and in life.

Most people prefer self-deception to self-discovery because they cannot overcome the discomfort of discovering possible deficiencies in their auto-self. The thought of plumbing the murky depths of their embedded self-image terrifies most people. I have witnessed powerful personalities with substantial success histories cower at the prospect of meeting their auto-selfs. These people seem to equate their self-worth or security with viewing themselves favorably, even if inaccurately.

Comfort priorities that conflict with success priorities, and prevail, do so at a debilitating cost. The inability to embrace self-discovery deprives people of the opportunity to recognize their shortcomings mixed among their excellent characteristics. This often leads to blindsided career derailment and equally devastating problems in their personal lives. In common with other auto-contexts, our self-image resists change through avoidance and denial. Unfortunately, this often creates a blockage to traversing the first step of auto-self improvements.

Aversion to self-discovery is part of human nature. Why? Our self-image is deeply ingrained in an auto-context. Reconstructing an auto-context almost always creates discomfort, and that is particularly true when the auto-context defines who we are to ourselves.

Any external evidence that contradicts our self-image creates an internal reality war.

The **Recontextualizing Principle**

Reconstructing auto-contexts, or *recontextualizing*, often creates as much discomfort as *transforming* auto-behaviors. As with behavior change, recontextualizing requires erasing and replacing a deeply ingrained auto-self structure. The process requires that we uncover (make explicit to our thinking-self) a hidden auto-context that appears to us as the way things really are, consciously replace it with a more serviceable alternative, and explicitly use it until it once again becomes an auto-context.

The **Counteracting Principle** is an overarching principle that underpins many of the techniques described in this book for transforming auto-behaviors.

Similarly, the **Recontextualizing Principle** is an overarching principle for many techniques for reconstructing auto-contexts. We use it sparingly in this book on auto-behavior change – namely for changing a self-image (creating static self-awareness) and reconstructing attitudes and expectations as a means of changing auto-behaviors. We will develop the Recontextualizing Principle much further in the next book in this series on our two-selfs.

You now understand what happens when we encounter an internal reality war – we reflexively take actions to avoid the discomfort.

In their struggle to escape the discomfort of the internal reality war, people employ every evasion gimmick they can, including denial. To counteract the discomfort of self-image change it is often necessary to employ a heavy dose of feelings-inducing techniques.

Jake's resistance to accepting his counterproductive behaviors brought him to the brink of derailing his career.

Does Jake Accept His Behavior Feedback?

"This is crunch time, Jake." – Alex

"I'm a self-made man," Jake said during one of our hour-long sessions. "I made myself everything I am today. I run on gut instinct and do what works."

"Are you sure that following your gut instinct is always the right thing to do?" I asked, knowing it was not a rhetorical question for him.

"It has always worked for me," Jake said. "I don't make bad decisions."

"Well, Jake," Cyril, his coach, pointed out, "it seems your gut instinct does not work all the time because you repeatedly can't get promoted beyond District Sales Manager. What do you think might be holding you back?"

He sat back for a moment, his face a mask of thought.

Rather than considering the uncomfortable possibility that he was doing things that undermined his own success, Jake looked outward, saying, "I don't know. Maybe, someone doesn't want me to get ahead."

Having interviewed Jake's superiors, Cyril challenged his defense. "That sounds like a lame excuse to me because your HR director, your boss, and your boss's boss want to promote you to upper management. Do you fear success?"

"Hell no! I live for it!"

Preparing the ground to test Jake's beliefs about himself, Cyril said, "All right, Jake, let's pretend I'm one of your employees. Pick a name."

Jake picked the name, "Dennis."

Cyril continued, "OK. I'm Dennis and I come into your office on Monday morning. Alex, the Vice President of Sales and Marketing needs a complex financial analysis report by Wednesday morning and Dennis is one of the few employees with the skill and expertise to get it done. Now, I'm Dennis and here is what I say, 'Jake, my father is having emergency surgery tomorrow and I need…'"

"Whoa. Wait a minute. Who will complete the financial analysis by Wednesday?"

"I thought Karen could do it. She's done it before and…"

"I've seen her work and she's not that good. I cannot let you take tomorrow off."

"But, this surgery is important and…"

"I don't want to hear it," Jake said and put his hands up. His face scrunched up a bit.

"But, Jake…I need this day off!" I said, raising my voice a bit.

"I don't care," Jake said, digging in his heels. "You have got to get your priorities straight. The company always comes first, and if it didn't, we may not have jobs."

Switching out of my role-playing, Cyril commented, "You have become so focused on taking the best path to short-term results that you have lost sight of the big picture. First of all, Dennis would not do his best work if he was worried about his father and feeling guilty he was not there to support him and help his mother through the ordeal."

"In this circumstance, Karen would probably do a better job. Also, you would lose Dennis's respect – you would probably end up with grudging compliance rather than his enthusiasm and energy, which you need to succeed in the long run."

Stepping up the intensity of my feedback, Cyril said, "Your repeated aggressive behavior and your cold-hearted approach to short-term results at any cost alienates you from your team and causes many of them to request transfers out of your department and some star performers to leave the company in frustration."

I then began to give Jake an overview of what he could do to address these issues. "I am going to help you understand that it is not just the results you achieve but also how you achieve them that will lead to long-term success."

"Some of your behaviors run counter to this company's management philosophy and core values. If we can get you through your counterproductive behaviors, the company will likely promote you to fill the next regional manager opening.

"I'm afraid that if you dig in and refuse to change, you may face having to take your involuntary dysfunctional behaviors to another company."

Jake looked pensive and for a second we thought we had gotten through to him, but then he said, "I'm still not convinced I have a problem."

Undaunted by this familiar form of denial as a defense mechanism, Cyril explained, "Well Jake, you're in a state of denial about your auto-self. Two properties of the auto-self are that our actions take place outside of our awareness and they take place independent of our intentions. If we don't intend to do something and we don't notice when we do it, it certainly appears to us that we do not do it."

"However, we should pay attention to consistent feedback from several people who work closely with us and who know us very well. Before we start the transformation process, we must get you to a point where you recognize you have negative involuntary behaviors you need to change."

Later that day, Cyril reported his progress with Jake to his HR director, Lori, and they initiated an escalation plan to help Jake get through his aversion to accepting his shortcomings.

The following day Lori called Jake into her office and asked him, "Well, Jake, how is it going with the transformation coach?"

"OK, I guess," Jake replied noncommittally.

"Well, let me tell you. Your coach says you are resisting this like a stubborn mule. We don't want to think of you as a mule, but if you don't get through this program successfully, if you don't open up to it, you won't get that promotion," Lori bluntly explained.

Confronted with this coordinated challenge, Jake became jittery.

"Jake, you need to open up to your issues immediately. A coach's job is to help people change when they want to but cannot do it on their own. Your coach will terminate this engagement soon if you don't show a desire to change," Lori warned.

"You're serious about this?" Jake said with a tone of resentment.

"Damn right!" Lori immediately and unabashedly replied. "So if you don't straighten up…well you know the consequences."

Jake frowned. "I lose a handful of bad apples and I have to put up with this crap!"

"There were no bad apples, Jake," Lori countered, refusing to indulge his rationalization. "You had top-notch employees and some of them left the company because of you. You see, Jake, your behavior has not only hurt those employees, it has also hurt the company."

We cannot eliminate the discomfort associated with discovering and changing undesired habits, but we can employ techniques to counteract our natural resistance to self-discovery in order to enhance our chances of success.

Upping the ante, Alex, the Executive Vice President of Sales and Marketing, entered the room. Jake's stomach churned and he started to sweat. Alex was Jake's boss's boss and he looked serious. Alex asked Lori how things were going with Jake's coaching.

Lori responded, "Jake's at a crossroad because he still is in denial about the behaviors we want him to improve. His coach is about to terminate Jake's coaching engagement because Jake hasn't yet accepted that he has habits he needs to change."

Alex then turned to Jake and laid it on the line for him. "Jake, we all appreciate your hard work and dedication to the company and the results you have achieved. I would like to promote you to a regional sales manager reporting directly to me when the next opening comes up, but you will have to correct a few of your undesirable behaviors including two showstoppers – your all too frequent anger outbursts and your lack of empathy and support for your team."

Alex continued, directly confronting Jake's problematic behaviors, while simultaneously offering him support. "I want to be as clear with you as I possibly can, Jake, so you understand the choice you face now. I don't believe we can build a long-term successful organization using aggressive behaviors or lacking empathy for our employees' occasional personal issues. Beyond that, our CEO and executive staff have articulated a set of core values that some of your behaviors violate. Because we appreciate your considerable talents and would like to leverage your abilities in a higher-level position, we are willing to invest in a coaching program for you to help you overcome your bad habits. However, you have to acknowledge the behaviors that your management, the 360° (boss, peers, and subordinates) leadership survey, and interviews consistently identified."

Alex continued to play out the counteracting scenario he had rehearsed. "This is crunch time Jake because you will not just miss the promotion that you and the company would like to see happen, but I'm afraid we will have to out-place you if you don't immediately accept the feedback on your unacceptable behaviors."

Lori later told us, "At this point, Jake's face contorted and he turned pale. I got nervous; he seemed to stop breathing. I thought he might scream at Alex, throw up, or pass out. However, to Jake's credit, he maintained his composure, but he couldn't seem to make eye contact with either Alex or me."

Alex then pivoted to the reward side of the counteracting principle. "However, if you recognize the issues we want you to change and engage actively with your coach, your promotion will be a slam-dunk. You cannot change what you don't recognize and acknowledge. We have worked with this coach before and he always transforms behaviors in people he coaches who want to change. Spend a day or two looking over your feedback and dealing with the discomfort of acknowledging some shortcomings. When you decide whether or not you can accept the feedback, let Lori know and we will all know where we go from there."

At our suggestion, Alex applied strong techniques to counteract Jake's barrier to accepting his feedback. He

pushed Jake by creating huge discomfort by threatening termination, which we anticipated would cause Jake to accept his deficiencies as the path of least discomfort.

Alex also **pulled** Jake through his blockage by essentially offering him a promotion if he acknowledged his issues and engaged in coaching to correct them. This used pleasure to counteract self-discovery discomfort.

We normally avoid using such strong counteracting techniques, but repeated warnings to Jake that he would probably not achieve his promotion had not caused him to accept that he had serious deficiencies.

This strong technique, executed effectively by Alex, worked as expected. Jake came into Lori's office the next morning and told her, "Wow, did I spend a tough night last night. Fortunately, my family was supportive but they also told me they agreed with most of the assessments of my behavior. It is difficult for me because I don't really notice myself doing these things, so it doesn't seem to me that I actually do them. However, my coach explained about the automatic mode we all sometimes work in, so I guess I don't have to feel like I was deliberately acting like a jerk because it was all unintentional.

"Now I'm worried that I won't be able to change these behaviors even though I acknowledge them, because I don't really notice when I do them."

Lori responded, "Jake, I'm delighted you decided to get on board and proceed with your coaching. Don't worry about noticing your behaviors. That's why we engaged a coach for you; he will coach you to notice and change them."

You can magnify the velocity of advancement by exploiting your unique strengths and capabilities, and you can avoid the trauma of derailment by overcoming any undesired behaviors and barriers to needed actions. However, these benefits require awareness.

Achieving static self-awareness. of counterproductive behaviors is the opening bid in the transformation process.

The next step is for the client to determine what he or she wants to achieve beyond what would have been currently possible. Then, the client identifies behaviors to change that will enable achieving these new goals.

13: Declaring Anchors for Change

*To lay a foundation for habit transformations, we anchor them in **goals** and **intentions**.*

We need to *convince* the *thinking-self* and *motivate* the auto-self. That is, we must understand what to do to succeed and become motivated to do it.

Some self-help authors assert that we can "choose" to do better. Our thinking-self chooses. Our auto-self does not pay much attention to such choices. We cannot <u>choose</u> to have our auto-self operate differently. We can, however, <u>choose</u> to become different and launch a guided effort to undergo the arduous process of transforming that aspect of our auto-self. We use *grand goals* as the mechanism to <u>choose</u> what we want to achieve. We use *intentions* to <u>choose</u> the behaviors we want to transform, using the guided-change process, to achieve those grand goals.

Grand Goals

"Grand goals create the framework and motivation for change."

In coaching, we normally have clients commit to achieving 2 to 5 "grand goals," which are usually stretch goals that exceed their normal business goals and sometimes include a personal goal.

Each grand goal must have a measurable or verifiable result, must have a fixed date for accomplishment, and must be unconditional. We never let clients sneak in conditions such as, "I think I will," or "I'll try," or "I commit to achieving this goal as long as other activities don't interfere."

When you help someone as a transformation guide, your client may have only one grand goal, but there may also be other goals related to overcoming the counterproductive behavior associated with the grand goal.

When Jeremy worked with Penny, he guided her toward declaring a health goal and a goal to improve her leadership ability at work. As a result, Penny created a grand goal to lose 50 pounds in one year and keep it off permanently and she decided she would improve the performance of her team at work by 20% within one year.

Grand goals create the framework and motivation for change. However, transformation coaching focuses on behavior change, so we must close the gap between goals and behaviors that impact achieving those goals.

Intentions

Intentions anchor the feelings that can counteract habit-change discomfort.

After they declare their grand goals, we persuade clients to declare *intentions* for new behaviors that will help them achieve their grand goals. These intentions provide the focal point for the transformation process. That is, the client declares intentions to stop the old counterproductive habits and identifies new productive behaviors that will replace them. The client also declares intentions to overcome old barriers to action and identifies the new empowering actions that will replace them.

Penny declared two intentions with regard to her health goal. She would avoid eating fried foods, desserts, other sweets, and junk food between meals. She also would exercise an average of 20 minutes per day indefinitely. For her work-related goal, she declared intentions to avoid micromanaging and to hold people accountable for meeting their commitments.

Principle: **Behavior-Change** *Anchors*

In order to keep the coaching process on track, have clients *declare* **grand goals** for what they want to achieve and **intentions** for behaviors they need to change to achieve those goals. These declarations work as *commitments* or *promises* that they make to themselves and to their guide/coach. When the going gets tough and clients try to resist the change process, guides can get them back on course using the path of least discomfort.

The Power of Declarations as Anchors

"Barry, stop working on your agenda. Focus on what I want to do!" – Ron

The following case study illustrates the power of declaring grand goals and intentions for keeping the coaching process on track. It also demonstrates the efficacy of understanding the counteracting principle by employing the path of least discomfort in a manner other than using deadlines.

Ron entered coaching due to excessive control issues and an unrelenting drive to win personally at everything – often at the expense of colleagues and his company.

Following our normal course for creating transformation anchors, Ron declared four *grand goals*. Consistent with his bold, winning style, he chose tough but doable goals to achieve by the end of our targeted one-year coaching engagement.

As usually happens, Ron struggled with the results he received from his leadership performance feedback that included an online 360° survey (his boss, peers, and direct reports) and interviews. To his credit, after working through the agony he experienced with some of the challenging feedback, he identified five auto-behaviors that he wanted to change in order to achieve his grand goals. He then declared explicit *intentions* to change each of his five undesired behaviors.

Ron embraced the coaching process and made steady progress. He became increasingly adept at noticing occurrences of the auto-behaviors he wanted to change (overcoming the natural barrier imposed by the auto-self, which operates outside normal awareness). With his new dynamic self-awareness, Ron was increasingly able to substitute his desired behaviors.

Ron diligently kept a log of his successes and failures related to his intentions. During our sessions, we focused on how he felt about enacting his intentions, and his strong pleasurable feelings would reinforce his ability to continue with the new behaviors. As normally occurs at the beginning of a coaching engagement, Ron also had quite a few misses. Because he took his declaration of intentions seriously, and because he believed enacting those intentions would enable him to perform at a higher level and achieve his grand goals, he faced up to his missed intentions and genuinely felt bad about them.

My coaching was working as intended.

However, one day we hit a critical point in our coaching engagement. Ron had gone through his successes and failures with his intentions, and we had moved on to discuss other activities that had taken place since we last met.

While Ron was recounting a frustrating meeting he had on Tuesday, he casually mentioned that he called Hank, one of his direct reports, "stupid" during a meeting. As soon as I found a break in Ron's monologue, I seized the initiative and said to him, "Ron, I want to go back to your meeting on Tuesday and your encounter with Hank. You said you called him 'stupid' in front of his peers."

"That's right, he said something really boneheaded. Now I want to go back to the meeting I felt really good about on Wednesday."

This time I did not wait for a pause in Ron's discussion. "Whoa, Ron," I interrupted. "I want to go back to your meeting on Tuesday. How do you feel about what you said to Hank?"

"I feel fine," Ron defended. "Hank deserved it." Ron then attempted again to shift the conversation to a more comfortable subject, saying, "Now can I continue telling you about how well I did on Wednesday?"

I responded: "I want to hear about your Wednesday meeting, Ron, but right now I want to focus you on the Tuesday meeting with Hank."

"Barry, stop working on your agenda. Focus on what I want to do!" Ron barked at me.

Such aggressive behavior creates discomfort, even for an experienced coach, but seasoned coaches have conditioned themselves to avoid the normal auto-self-driven fight-or-flight response to aggressive behaviors from their clients. It obviously will not do to hang up or scream back at your coaching client.

Although I experience discomfort, I have no problem remaining outwardly calm with aggressive clients; yet plotting a powerful next move in real time while under duress can create a challenge. However, I had seen this evasion pattern many times and I knew exactly what I wanted to do next.

"OK, Ron," I said, "Take out your list of intentions and explain to me how your behavior was consistent with Intention #3 – 'I will treat everybody with respect.'"

As I normally do after asking an open question, I went silent. As the excruciating silence crept along, I could visualize exactly what Ron was doing. Even though this was a telephone session, I had been with him face-to-face on enough occasions that I knew in such situations he looked up at the ceiling with a serious look on his face while he pondered what to do next.

While waiting for Ron to resolve the internal reality war I had trapped him in, I wondered which path he would take to resolve it and I plotted some next moves depending on how he responded. Frequently, clients will resort to an evasion gimmick by creating elaborate excuses or rationalizations as to why they had not really violated an intention. I figured Ron was too perceptive to go down that path. As one former client said to a coaching prospect of mine who interviewed him as a reference, "One of the powerful techniques that Barry uses to force us to face our dysfunctional behaviors is to strip away our rationalizations relentlessly."

After what seemed like an eternity, Ron finally said, "I guess it is not consistent."

To his credit, Ron avoided rationalizing the behavior. Was he now ready to face the counterproductive behavior he had exhibited and work on changing it?

I continued to push the point. "So what are you going to do about it?"

After struggling for quite a while to find a way to escape the internal conflict in which he found himself enmeshed, he finally growled, "I will just drop Intention #3."

I have clients declare explicit intentions so that they will experience pleasure when they enact them and discomfort when they violate them. This process eventually leads to transforming their counterproductive habits. Unfortunately, the discomfort of addressing this counterproductive behavior was too great for Ron, so he chose to drop one of his intentions.

I responded by leading him into a follow-up dilemma. "It is not for me to determine your intentions, Ron, so drop Intention #3 if you like. Now please pull out your list of grand goals. How likely is it that you will achieve Grand Goal #2 regarding having a motivated and energized team if you delete Intention #3?"

After another pregnant pause, his well-honed rational calculations took over and he admitted, "It is unlikely."

I now had Ron where I wanted him and I said, "All right Ron, what is your next move now?"

I had escalated the consequences for Ron. If he continued to justify his dysfunctional behavior, Ron would have to abandon one of his grand goals, which I knew was vitally important to him.

After another long, agonizing delay, he said rather meekly, "I want to keep Intention #3. Yes, I violated it, and darn you for trapping me so I couldn't skate by this one."

As the tension eased a bit, we discussed what had just happened, and Ron agreed that avoiding that particular behavior was his agenda, not mine, and I was just making it difficult for him to rationalize ("Hank deserved it") his counterproductive behavior that he found difficult to stop.

This exchange also illustrates why self-help behavior changes normally fail to produce the desired results. Most of the time people use evasion gimmicks to fool themselves in a reflexive effort to avoid the inevitable discomfort of transformational change. They tell themselves anemic stories that enable them to quit their self-help effort without feeling bad about their failed attempts at improving.

During our next coaching session, Ron said he had reviewed some of the material I previously sent him. He asked if I deliberately led him into a trap that would force him to admit he had behaved poorly because that was the path of least discomfort out of his internal reality war. I affirmed his suspicion. He asked why I did not tell him during the session that was what I was doing.

I explained that discussing the auto-self and various transformation techniques *at the beginning* of a coaching engagement could help a client understand auto-behavior and auto-context activities, some techniques that can transform them, and the discomfort that normally accompanies the transformation process.

In addition, a *retrospective* discussion, such as we were having after Ron successfully resolved his internal reality war in favor of positive transformation, can help clients understand what happened. This can help them leverage the process for future personal changes or possibly use it while serving as a transformation guide for others as happened with Jeremy who was guiding Penny.

However, *during* the process, one must experience it, not think about it, for it to create the desired result.

Ron got it. He volunteered some appreciation, "It really helps me to understand the existence of the auto-self. I don't think I could make sense out of what happened to me without those insights."

Ron also offered his observations about our last session. "The previous coaching session was a turning point for me. I struggled with it the last couple of days. I had to face the fact that I was rationalizing a deep-seated behavior that I found difficult to change, and I came out feeling confident I now can change all of my unwanted auto-behaviors."

Ron then made a good-natured parting observation. "Although the process helped me greatly, I hope we never have to repeat it because it felt like crap." Such is the nature of transformational change.

The situation with Ron is similar to many others I have encountered. Declaring grand goals and intentions puts stakes in the ground for anchoring transformational change. Grand goals provide the reason to change and produce a backstop if sliding occurs on fulfilling intentions.

Explicit declarations of intentions for new behaviors can create both positive and negative feelings to counteract the normal human tendency to avoid the discomfort of transformational auto-behavior change.

Ron went on to transform the five counterproductive behaviors that he indicated in his intentions. He also achieved three of his four grand goals on time, and he completed the fourth one just one month late. Understandably, Ron is extremely proud of the improvements he made to some of his counterproductive habitual behaviors. As a result, Ron is confident he will move soon to the next level of management.

I also take great joy in having helped Ron achieve his goals by changing his dysfunctional habits that blocked his way to greater success. Helping people to perform beyond what they or others thought possible, such as happened with Ron and many others, makes me happy that I chose to retire my executive role to become a transformation coach.

You, too, can enjoy the fruits of this effort, both through your improved performance and in the form of satisfaction of guiding others to overcome their barriers to success.

Technique:
Declaring Behavior-Change Anchors

What This Technique Means:
Anchors are *declarations* that put stakes in the ground for the behavior transformation process.

How to Use This Technique:
Guide clients to declare unconditional, time-specific, result-specific goals and intentions for behaviors needed to reach those goals.

Why This Technique Works:
This is another technique that implements the counteracting principle. Declarations create an internal and external commitment to achieve something or act in a certain way. Stripping away evasion gimmicks forces the client to face a fundamental deficiency. The concomitant discomfort serves to counteract the auto-self resistance to the change. The pleasure of meeting a commitment also counteracts the resistance to change.

Jake Declares His Anchors

"Now you're rolling, Jake."

The next time Cyril met with Jake, he appeared a lot different from previous meetings. He looked vulnerable and open to solutions to his problems.

Even his body language had changed – he no longer sat in the chair like a king on a throne.

Cyril took advantage of this critical opening and said, "Jake, Lori tells me you have accepted the major issues identified in your leadership survey and that you are ready to dive into your coaching program. I'm delighted. With your obvious talents and ability to deliver results, you will be a true star performer once you transform your undesirable behaviors."

"We can now focus on your grand goals. You previously identified achieving the promotion to regional sales manager within one year. The goal is already in the correct form of having a verifiable result and a specific date. What other grand goals would you like to achieve during our one-year coaching engagement?"

"I've been thinking about that," he replied, "and I would like to become better and more comfortable at public speaking. You probably wouldn't guess it from my strong personality," Jake courageously confided, "but I get extremely nervous when I speak before large audiences, so I avoid it like the plague. Also, since I rarely speak publicly, I don't think I have developed very good presentation skills. I don't understand why I get so nervous in front of large crowds. I have no problem at all speaking in front of a few customers in a small conference room. I think that to perform effectively at the next level I will need to do more public speaking, so I want to get better at it."

"Jake, the public-speaking phobia is very common," Cyril told him. "I suspect it's an evolutionary maladaption to retreating in the face of a large, hostile group. To make this one of your grand goals, you need to formulate it with a measurable or verifiable result in a fixed timeframe."

Cyril paused to allow Jake time to figure out a powerful formulation.

"How about this? By the end of one year I will have given four presentations in front of large crowds."

"That works, Jake. Do you have any other grand goals for yourself at work?"

"I've tried to think of other goals, but nothing occurs to me now. Is it possible to add another grand goal if I think of one later?"

Cyril was happy to accommodate Jake's request. "Of course – clients often come up with additional goals as we work our way through intense discussions on what it takes to succeed."

Shifting gears, Cyril asked, "How about any personal goals outside of work?"

"I've been thinking about that also," Jake disclosed, "but I'm afraid the company would not like spending money on improving my personal goals. Although I apparently have many faults, acting unethically is not one of them. I think I would need to ask them for permission, and I really don't want to discuss my personal issues inside the company."

Jake's concern was understandable, but his coach was able to offer reassurance because the overall coaching process is helped, rather than hindered, by addressing goals in different aspects of the client's life (as discussed in Chapter 19: Leveraging Auto-Self Experiences).

"Don't worry about that, Jake. Lori knows we have helped other leaders accomplish personal goals such as stopping smoking and losing weight and keeping it off by establishing healthy eating and exercise habits. We will interact twice a week for the next year. During that time, we will have opportunities to fit in a personal issue for you without negatively affecting your progress on the company issues. Besides, a healthier, happier employee is usually a more effective employee, so achieving a personal goal will likely also help the company."

"Depending on the nature of your personal goal and your feelings about it," Cyril noted, "we can either tell Lori and Alex or not. You make the decision. In addition, we will not disclose any personal or business details we discuss that you want to keep private. As you know, we will give quarterly progress reports to Lori and Alex. However, we report on progress in general terms and usually avoid specific instances. We promise you confidentiality on any issues that you identify as sensitive, and we will use our judgment to avoid discussing other potentially sensitive issues even if you don't flag them."

Put more at ease by those safeguards, Jake opened up, saying, "OK, here it goes. When I met with my wife, son, and daughter to discuss issues identified in my leadership survey, they suggested that if I needed to be more sensitive to the personal lives of my team that maybe I could work on becoming more sensitive to the needs of my own family. That was painful to hear. However, if I'm going to dive into this coaching thing and struggle to change myself, I guess I should listen to my family's feedback as well."

Cyril then reinforced Jake's brave disclosure of this vulnerable information. "Now you're rolling, Jake. You have become more open to feedback on your involuntary behaviors and you seem determined to maximize the benefits of your coaching experience. There will be times during the next year when you face uncomfortable changes, but by the end of the year you will feel exhilarated and empowered because you will have much greater control over your life and be surrounded by happier people." Easing him forward, I then said, "Now try to formulate your personal goal in the standard format."

Jake had already thought about this because he immediately responded, "I pledge to attend at least one school event every month for both of my children and to take my wife out somewhere once a week."

"Those are great pledges Jake," Cyril encouraged, "but they are your intentions for behavior changes, not your goal. How would you like to formulate your personal goal?"

After a long pause while he tried to formulate an effective goal, Jake finally stated, "How about this? At the end of one year, I will sit down with my family again and ask them if I have met their expectations for improving my participation in our family life. The verifiable result will be that all three of them say 'yes.'"

"That's a wonderful and brave goal for you to take, Jake," Cyril replied enthusiastically. "Now you not only have your personal goals but you also have three specific intentions related to that goal – if you count your participation in each child's activities as a separate intention."

Switching back to Jake's professional aspirations, Cyril urged, "Now let's work on your intentions for your two business grand goals." Jake summarized his progress and challenges, saying, "I've done some work on my intentions related to getting promoted to regional manager. However, I don't have a clue how to formulate intentions for my public speaking goal."

"Here are my intentions for my promotion goal:

1. Avoid anger outbursts except in the most egregious situations.
2. Show more empathy for my employees.
3. Get to know my team better on a personal level."

"That's a good start Jake. Your first intention is clear and you should be able to monitor success or failure. You are on the right track with Intention #2, but it is not yet in a usable form. It would be very hard for you to log whether or not you were showing empathy – the formulation is too vague. Your third intention is more like a goal. It usually takes a few sessions to hone the goal statements and intention declarations for maximum effectiveness." Cyril then asked him to think about his goals and intentions some more between sessions and told him they would discuss them again when they met next.

Cyril then gave Jake a suggestion to facilitate his thinking on the issues they had identified. "One intention I recommend you consider for your presentation goal is to join and actively participate in a Toastmasters International group near you. You will find a friendly environment where you can get practice giving formal presentations in front of a group that will give you support and constructive feedback on how to make improvements. With lots of practice, people normally begin to overcome their fears of presenting to groups. If, after you alleviate your fear of speaking, you want to develop further skills, I know of an excellent professional workshop series I can recommend to you." Cyril then encouraged Jake to think of other intentions that they could work on during their coaching sessions.

Looking ahead, Cyril told Jake, "The next step in the coaching process is for you to log successes and failures of enacting your intentions. We have you do this so that you will begin to notice how you do with your intentions and so that we will have these events to discuss at our coaching sessions. Between now and our next session, please focus on logging how you do on your first intention for your promotion goal. If you get angry, log it. If you feel yourself starting to get angry but you avoid it, log that also. In these cases, as with all occurrences of behaviors associated with your intentions, do your best to feel great when you enact your intention and to feel poorly if you fail to enact your intention. Experiencing these feelings may challenge you at first because they go opposite to your normal feelings, so I will help you work on those feelings during our sessions. Repeatedly experiencing discomfort with the old behavior helps to extinguish it. Repeatedly experiencing pleasure with your new behavior helps to establish it."

Jake was off to a great start. As we anticipated, once Jake cleared the enormous hurdle of accepting his shortcomings, he threw himself into the coaching process with the same gusto that he throws himself into succeeding at his job.

Gaining Perspective on the Transformation Process

The following diagram provides a perspective on the habit-change process and shows where chapters fit into the overall process.

The habit-change process starts at the top of the diagram. The arrows in the diagram indicate the flow of coaching activities.

The Habit-Change Process

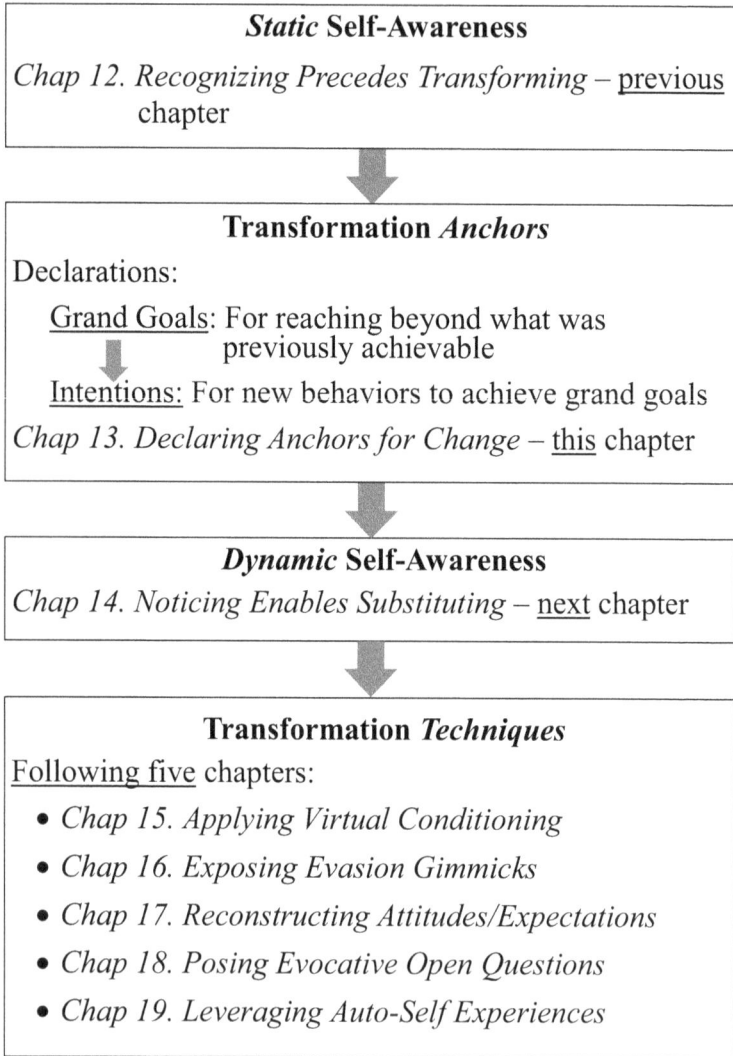

Static Self-Awareness

Chap 12. Recognizing Precedes Transforming – <u>previous</u> chapter

---

Transformation *Anchors*

Declarations:

Grand Goals: For reaching beyond what was previously achievable

Intentions: For new behaviors to achieve grand goals

Chap 13. Declaring Anchors for Change – <u>this</u> chapter

Dynamic Self-Awareness

Chap 14. Noticing Enables Substituting – <u>next</u> chapter

Transformation *Techniques*

<u>Following five</u> chapters:

- *Chap 15. Applying Virtual Conditioning*
- *Chap 16. Exposing Evasion Gimmicks*
- *Chap 17. Reconstructing Attitudes/Expectations*
- *Chap 18. Posing Evocative Open Questions*
- *Chap 19. Leveraging Auto-Self Experiences*

The transformation process starts with helping the client to achieve *static* self-awareness – that is, to *recognize* auto-behaviors that interfere with greater success, which the previous chapter described. .

After recognizing auto-behavior activities that undermine greater success, the client then reaches for grand goals and declares intentions to change behaviors to achieve those goals. That was the topic in this chapter.

The next chapter introduces the concept of *dynamic* self-awareness that we achieve when we *notice* or *observe* our auto-behaviors as we enact, or fail to enact, them. Because we do not normally notice what our auto-self does, the next chapter is also where we must start to dig into the actual inner-workings of our two-selves in order to create dynamic self-awareness.

The bottom box on the diagram identifies the actual techniques to use to change a behavior once we recognize it, declare that we want to change it, and learn to observe the undesired auto-behavior while we enact it. Whereas the previous steps all flowed in a sequence, transformation coaches and guides can mix and match the techniques in this box (no arrows) as dictated by the needs of the client and the situation.

14: Noticing Enables Substituting

We must somehow overcome this natural barrier to noticing our habitual behaviors.

This is the problem Jake worried about when he finally faced his counterproductive behaviors: how would he ever learn to notice his bad habits that he never even knew existed?

Principle: *Dynamic* Self-Awareness

Unlike the *recognizing* type of self-awareness (*static* self-awareness), which is a one-time "ah ha!" event, the *noticing* type of self-awareness is an ongoing introspection process of people attempting to observe each occurrence of the behavior they want to change. Accordingly, we call this type of awareness "*dynamic* self-awareness."

The main barrier to achieving static self-awareness, or recognizing that we have an auto-self characteristic (often an undesired habit) we may want to change, is a latent fear that feedback received might conflict with our (auto-context maintained) self-image.

We encounter a very different problem with achieving dynamic self-awareness. Discomfort does not block us from achieving dynamic self-awareness. Instead, one of the fundamental properties of the two selfs creates the barrier to observing our auto-behaviors. Our thought streams (sometimes referred to as "streams of consciousness") in the form of interpreting or telling stories normally consumes our thinking-self so "we" do not naturally notice our auto-self's activities. That works out very well for us most of time because we count on our auto-self to handle all of our routine activities without us having to give them a thought. However, when we have an auto-self characteristic that undermines our success, we must somehow learn to notice it as it occurs so that we can substitute a new, more functional activity.

The key to learning how to notice unwanted auto-self events and to transform them is to understand the properties, or the inner-workings, of our two mental modes. I have identified many two-selfs properties, and I describe eight of the properties in this book that are particularly useful in achieving dynamic self-awareness and transforming undesired auto-behaviors. Appendix B summarizes the eight two-selfs properties described in this book.

We have already discussed two crucial auto-self properties. We center our view of our two selfs on Property #1: Our auto-self operates automatically; it operates independently from our desires or intentions and often in opposition to them. The second property of the auto-self is the one that concerns us here: its activities occur outside of our normal awareness. We must somehow overcome this natural barrier to noticing our habitual behaviors. The other component of this dual-mind property is that the thinking-self creates our awareness. In fact, it normally exhausts our awareness.

Principle: **Two-Selfs** *Properties*

Unlike auto-self *characteristics*, which are specific to an individual (such as habitual procrastination or uncontrollable anger), auto-self and thinking-self *properties* describe the way these two modes operate at a fundamental level. Identifying these mental properties enables us to transcend previous metaphoric insights into the automatic and thinking modes so that we can describe and understand them at a level sufficient to build reliable techniques for transforming people to become who they want to be.

To summarize, here are Two-Selfs Properties #1 and #2

Two-Selfs Property #1: **Control**

Automatic, involuntary, robot-like

Intentional, voluntary, thought/story-based

You can understand this property of the auto-self by thinking about urges, compulsions, phobias, procrastination, anger outbursts, driving, using a mouse, keyboarding, facial expressions, and resistance to transformation.

> ## Two-Selfs Property #2: **Awareness**
>
> Operates outside normal awareness
>
> Center of awareness; consumes awareness

This two-selfs property often causes blindsided career derailments. People focus on perfecting their knowledge-based activities and fail to notice and develop their automatic activities. Sometimes people fail to execute tasks in a timely manner or take actions necessary to lead their team. Other times leaders get everything done but do it in a manner that disrupts the organization and causes considerable collateral damage.

This property also blocks us from recognizing when we do things that annoy other people. We do not notice our auto-behaviors, but those around us do and they often experience our bad habits in unpleasant ways.

We have reached the point where we need to understand additional properties of our dual mind to enable us to overcome the inherent "noticing" limitation. Since the thinking-self normally misses what the auto-self does, we need to search for new ways to overcome this limitation if we are to learn to notice so we can initiate behavior changes.

> Two-Selfs Property #3: **Simultaneity**
>
> Many processes execute simultaneously
>
> Single task (thought, story) at a time

You can understand the thinking-self part of this property by noticing that you cannot read two stories at the same time, write one story and speak a different story at the same time, or tell a story and listen to a story at the same time. Our thinking-self is very limited this way. However, it can process extremely complex "stories" including mathematical formulas, scientific theories, musical compositions, manufacturing processes, and the plots of dramas – including our own life dramas.

The auto-self, on the other hand, can process many activities in parallel including such things as facial expressions, gestures, voice inflection, sentence parsing, and language understanding. The image below illustrates this point using steering a car, noticing a traffic signal, listening to music, tipping a drink up to your mouth, and working the pedals all at the same time.

Many Auto-Self Processes Operate Simultaneously

Telling or understanding stories normally consumes our thinking-self, so it has no capacity left to notice what the auto-self takes care of automatically. Since the auto-self handles many tasks simultaneously, it seems like our best hope to notice internal and external events that elude our thinking-self. Fortunately, auto-self Property #4 provides just the capability we need.

Two-Selfs Property #4: **Detection of Events**

Can detect many external and internal events

Misses most external and internal events

If we are at a party where several people around us are talking, we must focus on just one conversation, so the rest of the conversations become background noise. Our thinking-self misses most of what goes on even though we are close enough to hear other conversations.

Our auto-self is much more attentive to multiple activities. For example, while driving, our auto-self can notice a light change even when our thinking-self is busy talking. Our auto-self can simultaneously detect if we are moving too close to a lane line or approaching too near to the car in front of us and make automatic adjustments without having to involve our thinking-self.

The auto-self can detect many internal and external events. However, detecting an event is not yet sufficient. For us to notice it, our thinking-self must stop processing the single thought stream that currently occupies it and switch over to pay attention to the event. Fortunately, our dual mind has yet another property that meets this requirement.

Two-Selfs Property #5: Redirected Thoughts

Can redirect thought stream ("daydreaming;" sudden, acute notice of environmental events)

Gets redirected by auto-self (often unnoticed)

The auto-self can redirect the thinking-self. It happens when we "daydream" or when our mind "wanders."

You might notice this redirection when someone is talking to you, you are attending a lecture, or you are watching a movie and your thought process disconnects from the scene in front of you and starts processing an internal story related to the topic you were observing. Our auto-self recognizes something in the story and redirects our thinking-self. This property helps us learn new ideas by associating them with concepts that we already understand. We can make these properties more concrete by giving some examples.

A New Insight from a Confusing Reading Activity

Have you ever been reading, and all of a sudden your mind wanders off the story that you were reading; and when you return from the internal thoughts, your eyes are not focused on where you stopped paying attention to the story but are much further along? Did you wonder why that happened? That phenomenon makes no sense in the uniform-mind model that most people intuitively assume. You have probably noticed this quirk in your mental processing, but you lacked a viable model to understand it.

If we had a single-level mind, your eyes should remain focused where you stopped processing the story, so when you return from your internal thoughts you could continue where you left off. Here is what happens. While our thinking-self is off thinking about another topic, our auto-self keeps processing the written words and sentences. However, since the thinking-self can process only one story at a time, and since for a little while it is processing an internal story, the words the auto-self kept processing from the book had no thought process to receive them.

This phenomenon is also an example of high parallelism in auto-self processing. One of the processes of the auto-self noticed something in a story that was related to something else already known, and it sent the thinking-self off to think about it. The auto-self did this while it was processing the language for the reading-story that the thinking-self was processing. We do not normally "decide" to stop processing the story we are reading. In fact, we do not usually even notice that we go off to think about something related to the story. We only notice when we go back to read and realize our eyes are not at the same spot they were when our thinking-self left the book story to process an internal story.

Our auto-self routinely causes us to detach from the story in front of us to process an internal, and often related, story. In some cases, as with a book or a recorded video, we can go back and review the segment we missed. Occasionally, our mind goes off during a conversation. We could, but we often don't, tell the speaker we missed some of the conversation and ask the speaker to repeat it. In other cases, such as in a movie theater, a play, or in a large lecture hall, we just lost the part that went by when we were daydreaming.

In addition to providing an example of <u>sequential</u> *thinking-self* processing and <u>parallel</u> *auto-self* processing, this common activity is a powerful demonstration that we have two distinct components in our dual mind.

Detecting External Events

Some environmental events universally cause the auto-self to redirect everybody's thinking-self to pay attention. Experts have designed some redirecting signals in the form of traffic signals and emergency-vehicle sounds and sights. Evolution created one in the form of a baby's cry. Other times, repetition in our environment or our particular circumstances cause our auto-self to recognize the events of specific interest to us. These auto-self detections are deeply ingrained. For example, a child hollering "Dad!" still causes my auto-self to redirect my attention. When my thinking-self then processes the call, I realize it is a child's voice and my children are grown. I then return to my previous thought stream.

To create dynamic self-awareness, we must train our auto-self to detect specific behavioral events that we want to change such as anger outbursts for Jake or eating indulgently for Penny.

Try to recall instances when your auto-self recognized something in the environment and caused your attention to focus on it. Recalling and re-experiencing previous events can lessen your time to achieve dynamic self-awareness of behaviors you want to change (we develop this technique further in Chapter 19: Leveraging Auto-Self Experiences).

Selectively Detecting a Page

"Please pick up the white courtesy telephone."

The reading and other mind-wandering examples happen without explicit external events. Our auto-self detects a relationship and redirects us to an internal story, and we do not even notice that it happened. However, sometimes our auto-self detects an internal or external event and redirects our thought stream and we do not recognize it happened.

We understand mental events best when we experience and recognize them ourselves. Below is an example of my auto-self recognizing something important to me in the environment that interrupted my thinking-self.

This example of my auto-self detecting an external event occurred several years ago (before cell phones became ubiquitous) while I was at the Philadelphia airport. I was talking with some colleagues while waiting to board the plane. Talking to them and listening to them consumed my thinking-self. Suddenly my attention was diverted to the PA system. As I listened, a page came over the PA system for me: "Barry Borgerson, please pick up the white courtesy telephone." Remember, the two-selfs theory has nothing to do with mystical processes, so I do not claim to have a "premonition" auto-self process.

What happened was my ever-vigilant auto-self had done a pattern match on my name and interrupted my thinking-self so that I began to listen to the PA system. At the end of the announcement, it said, "this is a repeat message." By the time the announcer called my name the second time,

202 | Barry Borgerson

my thinking-self had disconnected from the conversation in front of me and started listening to the PA system, although I did not understand at the time how that happened.

The important thing to note here is that my auto-self recognized my name, and it caused my thinking-self to pay attention. Nobody else in my group heard the page. Their auto-self detector does not do a pattern match on my name.

The above event provides an opening to get our auto-self to notice the behaviors we want to change and interrupt our thinking-self so we can attempt to substitute our desired behavior.

Here is how it works: one of the simultaneously-acting processes (Property #3) of the auto-self detects (Property #4) the activity (the behavior we want to change, such as displaying anger or procrastinating) and alerts our thinking-self to notice it (Property #5).

What We Detect and What We Don't

Here is another example of how our auto-self processes external events. In this case, my auto-self did not redirect my thinking-self to pay attention to it.

While I was walking through a crowded area, I dropped something without realizing it. A woman noticed and attempted to get my attention with an escalating series of calls to me, "sir," "Sir," "SIR!" I did not respond but instead kept walking while staying in my reverie. Finally, she caught up with me and touched my arm. At that point, I was able to replay the three "sirs" in my mind and realize she had been trying to get my attention. My ever-vigilant auto-self had noticed her calls but had not alerted my thinking-self. Apparently auto-self processes that detect external-events have sophisticated filters that cause them to interrupt our thought stream when the event is fairly specific to us but not to alert "us" (our thinking-self) when the event is as general as calling out "sir."

My auto-self always interrupts my thinking-self when it detects one of my names: "Barry," "Borgerson," "Dad," "Uncle Barry," and "Pappy." It redirects my thinking-self from whatever scene it was processing to the source of the message. It did not interrupt my thinking-self for "sir," but when the woman touched my arm, an auto-self process that detects sensations redirected my thinking-self from the internal thought stream I was processing to pay attention to my environment including replaying her previous attempts to get my attention that my thinking-self missed.

There is another property of the auto-self that occurs when we use one auto-self process to detect another auto-self driven activity.

Two-Selfs Property #6: **Progression of Detection**

Can detect internal events progressively earlier

Does not progress in the time when it notices an event

In many cases, our auto-self first detects an undesired behavior *after* we display it. There is not much we can do at this point except apologize. Fortunately, Auto-Self Property #6 enables us to do better. If we keep practicing, we start to notice the targeted behavior *during* the event. At this point, we can interrupt ourselves and try to exit gracefully from the undesired behavior we just displayed. If we continue practicing, we can actually notice the undesired behavior *before* we start it and can substitute our desired behavior. A couple of examples should make this process clear.

Correcting a Grammar Mistake

Soon, I was noticing the mistake while I was in the process of making it.

A friend, Barbara, once pointed out to me that I was using an incorrect grammar construction. Since our auto-self constructs our grammar, I was unaware of this mistake and in fact was somewhat incredulous when first told about it. I asked Barbara to point it out immediately the next time she heard me use it. When she pointed it out, I was able to replay it in my mind and realize to my dismay (but not to my surprise) that I had indeed used it. I had achieved static self-awareness. of my minor grammar faux pas.

This was an opportunity to initiate an auto-self process so I could learn to notice this grammar construction in real time and substitute a better one. I arranged a private signal with Barbara so she could politely alert me if I used it in the presence of other people. After Barbara pointed out the grammar misconstruction to me a few more times, a new auto-self process emerged that detected the grammar mistake. That created dynamic self-awareness by alerting my thinking-self every time I made the mistake. I no longer needed help from my friend.

Originally, the interrupt that alerted my thinking-self took place after I had committed the mistake. That was obviously too late to correct the mistake, but at least I was dynamically aware that it occurred – I noticed it.

In a dramatic example of parallel auto-self processing, the detection process works at the same time as the process that creates the grammar.

Auto-self processing works very rapidly, so eventually the process that was noticing the mistake and alerting my thinking-self began to move earlier in time. Soon, I was noticing the mistake while I was in the process of making it, and I was able to stop in the middle, mumble a little, and restate the grammar construction correctly. My thinking-self, alerted by an auto-self process, was beginning to take control away for my auto-self grammar generator for that particular construction. Before long, I would notice the mistake before I started to speak, and I was able to substitute correct grammar without anyone noticing.

We can actually detect many internal events before we enact them in a way that is visible to the external world. What happened in this case is that one auto-self process recognized the grammar construction created by another auto-self process as it worked its way through an internal pipeline and before it got fully formed and ready for speech enactment.

After a while, it occurred to me that it had been a long time since my auto-self had interrupted my thought stream and caused my thinking-self to notice my errant grammar about to emerge. Was I back to making the mistake and just not noticing it? Or, had my grammar generation mechanism corrected itself?

To see how the latter process works, we can look to the seventh two-selfs property introduced in this book – emergence.

Two-Selfs Property #7: **Emergence**

Processes imperceptibly emerge to execute repeated activities automatically

Requires focused attention and effort

This two-selfs property identifies that anything we repeatedly do, often initiated by our thinking-self, automatically and imperceptibly migrates to an auto-self process that handles it outside of our awareness. For examples, think about keyboarding, using a mouse, driving a car, playing a sport or a musical instrument, and learning to control your hands, voice inflection, and eye contact while speaking publicly.

Returning to my story about my grammar mistake – I assumed that when I no longer noticed this particular grammar mistake that my repeated thinking-self substitution of the desired grammar construction eventually migrated to an auto-self process that replaced the old auto-self-based misconstruction.

It was also possible, however, that my auto-self process that recognized the mistake had somehow gone dormant and I was no longer noticing the misconstruction. Understanding the mind as I do, I felt confident it was the former case. It was not difficult, however, to verify the result. Not surprisingly, on a subsequent visit to my mother my auto-self alerted "me" (that is, my awareness-producing thinking-self) to her use of the same grammar misconstruction. It was now clear to me that my auto-self still recognized the misconstruction and that another auto-self process had imperceptibly emerged to take over that part of my grammar construction.

This example of an auto-self (more an auto-skill than an auto-behavior) transformation vividly illustrates the use of several two-selfs properties in observing and transforming the auto-self. However, it was such a small matter that there was insignificant discomfort for me. Most auto-behavior transformations will create significant discomfort.

Dynamic Self-Awareness: Gordon's Intimidation

He became able to abort his behavior while in the process of displaying it.

This is another example of the establishment of an auto-self detection process and its advance in time. This example has more feelings than the previous one, so the habit was not quite as easy to replace.

Technique:
Establishing *Dynamic* Self-Awareness

What This Technique Means:
This technique trains a coaching client to notice or observe an auto-behavior while it occurs.

How to Use This Technique:
Teach clients what to look for in the demeanor of people around them and have them practice until they notice a telltale nonverbal response to their own behavior. Another technique is to have a trusted person give a signal whenever you display the behavior you want to change as Barbara did for me and as I did for Gordon in the following story. In coaching, we make extensive use of a client's log to help create dynamic self-awareness (described below).

Why This Technique Works:
It works because it enables us to work around the limitations of Property #2 (Auto-self operates outside normal awareness) and Property #3 (Thinking-self processes just one task at a time) by understanding and using Properties #4-7 (Detection of Events, Redirected Thoughts, Progression of Detection, and Emergence) as illustrated in the examples in this chapter.

Gordon had reported directly to me in several different capacities. At the time of this intervention, he ran all product development activities for a business unit I headed. Gordon was an exceptionally talented engineering manager with a strong history of delivering products on schedule. However, repeated feedback indicated that he was bullying and intimidating colleagues and subordinates. When I presented Gordon with this feedback, he initially did not accept it. His behavior was not a thinking-self-based calculated technique to dominate others. An auto-self process occurring entirely outside of his awareness caused this behavior. Since intimidating people ran contrary to his basic values, he asked for help in recognizing it.

In order to identify instances of Gordon's intimidating activities, I started attending some of his meetings to observe his behavior. At one meeting, I saw Gordon lean across the table and hit his fist down when discussing a point with someone. He did not do it violently, but Gordon is a big, athletic man and was in a high-level position, so I could see how that action could intimidate. At the end of the meeting, I asked him to join me in my office. When we got there, I asked Gordon if he had noticed his intimidating behavior. He had not. When I described it to him, he could only vaguely recall having behaved that way. Since his auto-self drove his behavior and since it was quite a while between the event and when we met, his lack of connecting with it did not surprise me.

The second time we went through this process, Gordon was able to recall his behavior. This established a solid *static* self-awareness. for Gordon. He now *recognized* that he exhibited intimidating behaviors. Being the pro that Gordon is, he immediately declared an intention to change, and he was off and running to establish a workable *dynamic* self-awareness so he could *observe* his intimidating activities and then substitute more-appropriate behaviors. Each time he displayed such aggressive behavior in my presence, I would invite him to my office as soon as practical after the event and point out his behavior in detail. There were no threats to Gordon. This was just a gentle process of helping him become aware that he did display such behaviors, how he manifested them, and how often they occurred.

The discomfort that served to counteract his intimidating behavior was Gordon's own internal reality war. That is, when he became aware of his behavior, it was unacceptable to him because it violated his own values and his understanding of sound leadership behavior.

This is how the progression went. When I first pointed out his intimidating behavior, it surprised Gordon. Later, he reached the level of awareness such that my simply inviting him to my office at the end of a meeting became a trigger for him to recall that he had displayed an aggressive behavior again. A point came when Gordon preempted me and said he would like to see me after the meeting. Somewhere between the time he displayed the behavior and the end of the meeting he became aware of his action. Although still too late to avoid the intimidating behavior, he was now on his way to achieving the dynamic self-awareness that would launch his behavior transformation.

As he progressed, I would know when Gordon became aware of his aggressive behavior because he would look over to me and smile when he noticed it. There was no longer any need to have him come to my office. Gradually, the time between the behavior and his awareness of it shrank. The auto-self process that recognized his undesired behavior was progressing ever closer to the offending events.

To cut a long story short, Gordon's awareness progressed earlier in time to where he became able to abort his intimidating behavior while in the process of displaying it. Eventually, he became aware of it before he started and substituted his desired behavior without any display at all of his former aggression. I would always get a smile from him when he aborted an intimidating behavior, and later when he was able to avoid it altogether. His new behavior felt good to him because it was consistent with his values, which helped him establish it. As more time passed, this new behavior became automatic with Gordon. As normally happens, activities we initiate repeatedly with our thinking-self automatically migrate to an auto-self process. After I helped him notice his undesired behavior, Gordon changed his intimidating behavior on his own.

Self-help to change behaviors can work, often after receiving external help to achieve dynamic self-awareness, as the two examples above illustrate. However, in most cases, even after learning to notice the offending behavior, the discomfort associated with stopping the old behavior and attempting to substitute a new unfamiliar behavior creates such an impediment to change that people normally quit the process before achieving a transformation.

Gordon's behavior transformation process took about a year. Gordon had now complemented his already excellent execution abilities with a behavior profile that achieved even greater performance from his team. After my promotion to Group Vice President and General Manager of a large multinational business unit, I promoted Gordon to VP and GM of the business unit I had been running. He later went on to serve as a successful executive at a major parts supplier in the automotive industry.

Sidebar: **Two-Selfs and Mindfulness**

Dynamic self-awareness enables us to notice our behaviors and thought patterns that normally escape us. We use this technique as part of our transformation process that enables substituting a desired behavior.

Others have also discovered value in this form of introspection and have created techniques for other purposes. Buddhists use "mindfulness" as part of their religious practice. Some branches of psychology have developed secular adaptations of some Buddhist mindfulness techniques for psychotherapeutic purposes. Cognitive behavioral therapy employs a form of mindfulness. Jon Kabat-Zinn, founding director of the Stress Reduction Clinic and the Center for Mindfulness in Medicine, Health Care, and Society at the University of Massachusetts Medical School, has dedicated much of his life to bringing mindfulness into the mainstream of medicine and society.

Our endeavor here is new and specific. We leverage our understanding of thinking-self and auto-self properties to create a means to notice our auto-self's activities (creating dynamic self-awareness) that we want to transform for greater success at work and in life.

Relating "Competencies" to the Two-Selfs Model

Some observers have noted the following sequences of "competencies":

1. Unconscious incompetence
2. Conscious incompetence
3. Conscious competence
4. Unconscious competence

We can now understand these better within the two-selfs model of human activities.

Sequences of Competencies

Competencies	Two-Selfs Insight
Unconscious incompetence	Failing without static self-awareness Failure not recognized
Conscious incompetence	Recognizing failure with static self-awareness and possibly observing it with dynamic self-awareness
Conscious competence	Dynamic self-awareness Thinking-self takes control and substitutes desired behavior
Unconscious competence	Successful activity migrates to auto-self (Two-Selfs Property #7: Emergence)

Learning to Notice – Logging

After a few repetitions of this process, the client will normally learn to recognize behavior events.

Some people and organizations impose auto-self change (such as training a pet, political "brainwashing," and "cult conversions"). In coaching, we want clients to decide what to change and to participate in the transformation process. To do this, they need to notice the behavior they want to change so they can substitute a new desired behavior. I have argued that the best way to notice a behavior is to create a new auto-self process that does the detection and interrupts our thought stream. How do we create this new process? One way is to have someone alert us every time we enact the undesired behavior, such as Barbara did with me and I did with Gordon. However, that is not always possible or convenient. In particular, the coach or guide is normally not present in the environment enough to give the alert. Instead, the guide should have the client log instances of success or failure to change an undesired behavior.

Logging helps the dynamic self-awareness or observing process. It also can help the transformation process once we establish anchors in terms of an explicit intention for a behavior. We get what we monitor. That is, when we diligently measure or verify the results we commit to achieve, we strip away our ability to employ evasion gimmicks, which aligns our comfort priorities with our success priorities. We feel great when we enact our intention and we feel bad when we fail because we experience what we monitor.

Technique:
Logging Execution of Intentions

What This Technique Means:

Clients practice keeping a log, or journal, of successes and failures regarding each behavior they want to change.

How to Use This Technique:

Have clients keep an ongoing log of successes and setbacks in enacting desired behaviors. This log is a key mechanism for creating dynamic self-awareness of (learning to notice) the targeted behaviors and serves as the focal point during coaching sessions. After a brief exchange of pleasantries to reconnect, the first order of business in a coaching session is normally to examine the successes and failures of enacting intended new behaviors and to induce feelings appropriate to the success or setback.

Why This Technique Works:

If the thinking-self makes a concerted effort to notice the targeted behavior, after a few successful attempts the auto-self will take it over and do it automatically (Auto-Self Property #7: Emergence).

At first, the client will miss the targeted behaviors just as Gordon did. However, the guide should go over the log at every session and, if it is empty, have the client think back through all of the activities that occurred since the last session and search for instances of the undesired behavior. After a few repetitions of this process, the client will normally learn to recognize behavior events often after-the-fact but over time closer to the event and then eventually before the event occurs.

Most habitual behaviors have more feelings attached than the ones described above that we used primarily to illustrate the behavior-observing (dynamic self-awareness) process. In order to transform these more-tenacious habits, we need to employ counteracting techniques. The next five chapters describe *transformation techniques* that coaches and guides can select from to meet the needs of their clients.

15: Applying Virtual Conditioning

"Conditioning" to Change Human Behaviors

Induce the auto-self to create consequences rather than relying on the environment to provide them.

I have asserted repeatedly throughout this book that recognizing the dual nature of our mind and understanding some of the underlying two-selfs principles of operation, including the properties of the thinking-self and auto-self, opens up the next frontier for improving human performance.

The two-selfs theory helps us understand the large universe of automatic activities that we cannot control directly. These include our involuntary behaviors (habits, compulsions, personality traits), the hidden contexts (paradigms, mindsets, thought patterns, cultures, the "box") that frame our realities, and our automatic skills (sports, music, keyboarding, interpersonal, public speaking, motivational).

The two-selfs theory also enables us to understand and manage the two distinct driving forces (intentions created by our thinking-self; pleasure and discomfort driven by our auto-self) that create our success priorities and our comfort priorities, respectively.

> ## Principle: **Virtual Conditioning**
>
> This new powerful form of conditioning is extremely helpful when coaching people through behavior change. Unlike operant conditioning that works equally well on animals and relies on *real consequences* from the environment, **virtual conditioning** is unique to humans and relies on leveraging thinking-self intentions to instill feelings into the auto-self to provide *virtual consequences*.

We previously identified the two-selfs properties that enable us to enlist the auto-self to detect a normally unnoticed involuntary behavior while we are about to display it and then to interrupt our thought stream so we notice it (creating dynamic self-awareness of habits we want to change). Using these properties enables us to substitute a new behavior.

However, all of that is still not enough to effect a behavior transformation except in the easiest of cases.

Experiencing discomfort associated with trying to avoid a familiar but dysfunctional behavior (errors of commission) or trying to enact an unfamiliar, disliked action (errors of omission) creates such distress that most people give up trying and end up losing to the unfair fight.

We know from research by behaviorists in the psychology profession that rewards and penalties repeatedly applied to an animal can eliminate or extinguish an unwanted behavior or establish a desired behavior.

The psychologist most readers probably associate with this "operant conditioning" is B. F. Skinner who widely published the results of his experiments with animals. Most parents intuitively use this process in an effort to construct socially acceptable behaviors in their children. Transformation coaches and guides can learn from the research on operant conditioning but cannot normally use it directly.

Three significant issues with operant conditioning make this process unworkable for use by transformation coaches or guides.

Issue 1: Operant conditioning *imposes* change on the animal or person. Some clients ask me prior to starting a coaching engagement if they are in danger of having habitual behaviors transformed that that they do not want changed.

One client put it this way, "Barry, if I have aspects of my behavior that you don't like but I do, how do I keep you from changing those?"

I explained that the client actively participates in the transformation process and therefore is always in charge of what gets changed. We do not create "collateral damage" or unintended side effects. Transformation coaches enable clients to enact their own previously declared intentions.

Issue 2: The coach/guide is normally not present in the environment when clients display (or manage not to display) the behavior they want to stop, so it is not possible to apply consequences in close proximity to the events. The same holds true for overcoming barriers to action.

Issue 3: Operant conditioning fails to leverage a uniquely human capability – namely our thinking-self's ability to determine the behaviors we want to change and participate in the transformation process.

With operant conditioning, one has to wait for the client to *emit* a behavior. That will not do for us. Clients declare explicit intentions with respect to their behaviors/actions. Once they learn to notice the targeted events, they attempt to substitute their desired behavior. This transcends the work of operant conditioning, most of which was researched on animals, because animals have no way to declare intentions or to participate actively in the change process.

We can stop an instance of an unwanted behavior through willpower or by counteracting the feelings that drive it. However, attempting to oppose our comfort priorities on an on-going basis through desires and willpower alone is a losing proposition.

Principle: **Realigning Comfort Priorities**

The underlying mechanism to create a behavior transformation is to change a comfort priority to align it with a success priority (intention) so that the old, undesired behavior creates internal discomfort and the new, substituted behavior feels comfortable.

To transform an unwanted behavior, we need more from the auto-self process that detects instances of the behavior we want to change and redirects our thinking-self to notice it. We want the auto-self process that detects the undesired behavior also to create discomfort. This is the foundation of virtual conditioning – we induce the auto-self to create the consequences rather than relying on the environment to provide them. Fortuitously, the eighth and final two-selfs property introduced in this book provides this capability.

Two-Selfs Property #8: **Induced Feelings**

Can induce feelings based on external/internal cues

Normally operates free of strong feelings

One of the marvelous two-selfs properties (#7) is that activities repeatedly initiated by our thinking-self eventually migrate, automatically and imperceptibly, into an auto-self process. Our goal is to create a new auto-self process that does three things:

1. Detects an undesired behavior

2. Interrupts our (thinking-self) thought stream so we notice the behavior

3. Creates a negative feeling associated with the counterproductive behavior

We associate negative feelings with the old behavior whenever our auto-self detects it and we fail to substitute the new behavior. The negative feeling could come from such emotions as disgust, shame, frustration, humiliation, failure, embarrassment, or fright.

When we first attempt to substitute an unfamiliar behavior for the familiar but dysfunctional behavior, we normally experience discomfort because the new behavior seems "unnatural" for us. We want the new behavior to feel comfortable, so whenever we successfully substitute it, we need to induce pleasure. We can derive that pleasure from a number of specific emotions including satisfaction, accomplishment, and pride.

Virtual conditioning is such a big concept and powerful technique because it satisfies the three shortcomings listed above for operant conditioning in a coaching environment. It leaves clients in charge of what gets changed by having them declare explicit intentions for new behaviors. It substitutes *internally-generated* **virtual consequences** for *externally-produced* **environmental consequences**. It leverages the thinking-self's ability to create intentions and to take actions repeatedly until they migrate into an auto-self process.

This may all look very complicated with six two-selfs properties identified to effect virtual conditioning, but it is "under the hood." Fortunately, we are not repairing a hybrid automobile; we are driving the car. It helps to know about the two engines under the hood, but we are interested in how we can drive it to maximize gas efficiency. It helps the coach or guide to understand the sequence of processes involved in habit transformations, and it provides confidence for those of us who create new techniques that we build them upon a solid theoretical foundation.

However, the real interest is how to change unwanted behaviors.

Fortunately, the process is not as complicated as it may seem. In fact, some of these steps, including repeated activities migrating to an auto-self process and internal event-detection progressing forward in time, take place automatically by the auto-self without any effort on our part.

Insight: **The Nature of the "Future"**

The nature of the "future" may surprise you. The "future" is a story told in the present about something that may happen later. As such, the thinking-self creates stories about the "future," so it is a uniquely human phenomenon. The same is true for the "past," but we are particularly concerned with the impact that stories about possible future consequences have on current behavior. We fret or rejoice about the "past" and we worry about or eagerly anticipate the "future," but we live, we experience, we feel only at this moment.

"Today is the tomorrow you worried about yesterday."
– Dale Carnegie

"Today is the first day of the rest of your life."
– Anonymous

Virtual Consequences

Experience real feelings now to avoid the ramifications of actual consequences later.

Normally when we consider a potential benefit or penalty in the future (a thinking-self activity), it does not have the same effect as when we actually experience the consequences. That means that if we try to avoid an undesired (auto-self driven) habitual behavior or execute an uncomfortable (auto-self blocked) activity, we engage in an unfair fight. That is, we try to use thoughts about possible future consequences to overcome the intrinsic, immediate discomfort of changing a dysfunctional habit.

A powerful way to counteract the feelings that block transformational behavior change is to use "virtual consequences."

A transformation coach or guide induces *virtual penalties* by causing a person to experience, *in the moment, the discomfort that would likely occur later if the client fails to take the needed actions now*. Once we experience actual penalties associated with our dysfunctional behavior, it is usually too late to affect the outcome. The transformation helper also induces *virtual rewards* so that the client feels the pleasure now if the new behavior becomes the norm, which actually serves to make the new behavior become the norm.

This two-selfs view of the nature of the future explains why knowing that anger outbursts create failures at work and home doesn't cause most people to eliminate them, why widespread publicity surrounding the likelihood of contracting terminal cancer doesn't stop most people from smoking, and why the threat of long-term imprisonment or even the death penalty doesn't eliminate serious crimes.

Thoughts about future possible penalties usually do not create strong enough feelings to counteract the discomfort of habit change. People avoid the discomfort of contemplating possible future penalties by ignoring the topic or rationalizing that these consequences may not occur anyway.

Virtual conditioning creates transformational change by inducing counteracting feelings to translate the thinking-self *concept* of future *real consequences* into auto-self-induced *immediately felt virtual consequences*.

This is quite difficult to do for yourself, but an expert coach can induce these feelings. A transformation guide can induce virtual consequences by repeatedly having the client focus on the consequences of failure or success, *experiencing* what that would feel like, and associating these feelings with the old and new behaviors. This works for barriers to action and dysfunctional behaviors, and it works using both penalties and rewards. In fact, pushing and pulling simultaneously with virtual penalties and rewards usually produces the best results.

We can achieve our *future goals* only if we act appropriately (enact planned actions, avoid undesired behaviors) in an enabling series of *present moments*.

In summary, with virtual consequences we experience real feelings now to avoid the ramifications of actual consequences that will likely occur later if the dysfunctional habit is not broken.

Technique:
Instilling Virtual Consequences

What This Technique Means:
   Virtual consequences means instilling feelings in the auto-self regarding a current behavior that the client would likely experience later associated with continuing or changing the behavior at this moment.

How to Use This Technique:
   Identify something (thoughts about future consequences or a related topic that creates feelings) and associate the feeling with the behavior that the client wants to change. Repeated application of this technique will instill the feelings associated with the behavior into the auto-self.

Why This Technique Works:
   We can instill virtual consequences because we understand the properties of our two selfs. Instead of relying on the environment for *real consequences* (as with operant conditioning), virtual consequences provide the feelings that condition the change process. Dynamic self-awareness of the old and new behaviors, along with previously instilled *virtual consequences*, creates the counteracting feelings to transform the undesired behavior.

I have used virtual conditioning many times to help clients transform undesired habits. Chapter 22: Alan's Case: Putting it all Together describes one such example regarding overcoming destructive anger outbursts.

The following example describes applying virtual conditioning on a personal issue.

Chain Smoking Stopped

"Wow, now I realize what you mean by virtual consequences." – Don

While helping clients establish their businesses-related grand goals and intentions, I routinely ask them if they have any personal habits they would like to change while we spend a year working together.

Many people select a health habit such as to eat more sensibly, exercise regularly, or stop smoking.

One client, Don, was a long-term smoker in his early fifties who wanted to stop smoking but failed on all previous attempts (the unfair fight again). I decided that the best way to coach Don to overcome his smoking habit was to apply intense virtual conditioning.

While transformation coaching works well over the phone for most issues, instilling a heavy dose of virtual consequences to break a tough habit works best face-to-face.

Don worked halfway across the country from me, so I waited until my next monthly on-site coaching session. I showed him some heart-rending stories and horrific pictures of people suffering from the results of smoking.

One particularly moving picture showed an emaciated man nearing death from lung cancer with his wife and young son tearfully hugging each other at his hospital bedside while the man held a picture of himself playing with his son just a few weeks earlier.

I placed a pack of cigarettes next to the stories and pictures and I caused Don to experience feelings in the present that were realistic for him in the future if he kept smoking.

As I passionately described the real consequences this man and his family were experiencing, I watched Don grimace as he felt the effects of smoking and observed the man's family suffering. After inducing virtual penalties for quite a while, I switched to virtual rewards and focused on experiencing how much more stamina he would have and how he would be able to play with his grandchildren when they came if he stopped smoking.

These virtual consequences transformed a story about the hazards of smoking that might happen in the future into a powerful feeling experienced in the present.

After this intense experiential session, Don explained how it felt.

"Wow, now I realize what you mean by virtual consequences. I really felt the agony of that man's wife and son as they watched him wither away into a painful death. I experienced what it would feel like to put my family through such torment, in addition to my own excruciating pain. I also felt great about having improved energy and stamina. I think I will take up racquetball again."

It does not take many of these sessions to induce virtual consequences that break a bad habit. Don quit smoking! When I contacted him one year after our coaching engagement, he reaffirmed that he no longer smoked. While all of his previous attempts failed, virtual conditioning transformed Don's tenacious smoking habit.

Virtual conditioning provides a powerful tool to enable coaches (and guides) to transform dysfunctional habits in their clients. A fortuitous aspect of virtual conditioning techniques is that we can apply a minimum level of virtual penalties to break the old habitual behavior.

If the behavior is not too deeply ingrained, moderate virtual penalties suffice. Cases like Don's, of breaking an ingrained smoking habit, and Alan's (described later), of curtailing uncontrollable anger displays, require intensive use of virtual penalties.

Virtual conditioning is unique to humans and works most effectively when induced by a transformation helper. Virtual consequences help people change so they can avoid real consequences later. Virtual conditioning is just one of many auto-self change techniques that result from a clear understanding of the dual mind.

16: Exposing Evasion Gimmicks

Evasion gimmicks are stealth destroyers of sustained motivation to change.

We habitually use evasion gimmicks to avoid an activity that we experience as uncomfortable, whether or not we notice and acknowledge that discomfort. Transformation guides should expose these mental tricks as a powerful technique to keep a client on the habit-change path. Since we involuntarily use evasion gimmicks to fool ourselves, and often those around us, we are not likely to recognize and expose our own evasion gimmicks.

When clients explain why they did not enact an intention, learn to distinguish a bona fide *reason* from an evasive *excuse*. A genuine reason would be something that happened unexpectedly and out of the person's control.

Penny explained that she missed going to the gym for her regular exercise session one morning because she got trapped on the freeway due to a chemical spill when a tractor-trailer turned over. That was a valid *reason*.

On another day, she said she missed her workout because she woke up too late, had to iron a shirt, and needed to walk the dog. Jeremy told Penny that sounded like an *excuse*. She should have set her alarm to leave sufficient time to complete all those routine morning chores.

Your client will use, often without realizing it, a wide variety of evasion gimmicks. As the guide, you should keep your client on track by politely exposing these mental tricks. You can say something like the following:

"That sounds like an excuse to me."

"It seems to me like you are trying to substitute rationalization for what you need to do."

"You seem to take that action a lot when you have something more important to do. Do you think that might be one of your escape rituals?"

"Explain how that activity helps you succeed."

When we strip away evasion mechanisms, clients immediately experience the feeling of failure and encounter an internal reality war that normally helps counteract the feelings that caused them to fail in the first place.

Technique:
Exposing Evasion Gimmicks

What This Technique Means:
To avoid the discomfort of transformational change, most people involuntarily use mental tricks to evade the dual discomforts of the change process and of noticing they are failing to create the behavior change they desire. Transformation helpers can force the change process back on track by exposing their *evasion gimmicks* and focusing attention on the declared intention (a behavior-change *anchor*) to change.

How to Use This Technique:
Watch intently for use of the five forms of evasion gimmicks discussed previously and summarized at the end of this chapter. Politely but persistently point out to clients their use of any evasion gimmick.

Why This Technique Works:
This technique creates an *internal reality war* between the previously declared behavioral intention and the evasion of enacting it, which the guide can use to reestablish the change process through the *path of least discomfort*.

Discomfort Relentlessly Drives Us to
Evade the Arduous Habit-Change Path

We showed this image previously to illustrate how clients involuntarily charge toward a comfortable path to evade the discomfort associated with transformational change. The top image on the opposing page illustrates how a guide can prevent a client from faltering during the transformation process by exposing the consequences an evasion action.

Exposing evasion gimmicks, along with persistent support by the coach/guide, normally gets a client back onto the change path.

A Guide Can Expose Evasion Gimmicks

A guide can enable you to see the destruction that evasion gimmicks will cause and steer you instead to traverse the difficult transformation path to become a star at the peak of performance.

Transforming to Star at Peak of Performance

Reminder – Types of Evasion Gimmicks

Rationalization:	*Minimize importance:* Replace action with a story that action was not really needed
Procrastination:	*Keep putting off:* Acknowledge task – keep it low priority – be "too busy"
Escape Rituals:	*Divert attention:* Do something pleasurable when faced with uncomfortable task
Simplistic Solutions:	*Substitute:* Dodge needed action – take related action that does not achieve goal
Excuses as Reasons:	*Pretend: Excuse* away lack of action by pretending you have a real *reason*

Evasion gimmicks are stealth destroyers of sustained motivation to change.

Transformation guides must search for and expose evasion gimmicks relentlessly because their clients will use them.

17: Reconstructing

Attitudes/Expectations

Sometimes the way we view people or situations creates our behaviors.

Most of the behavior transformation techniques described in this book rely on the **Counteracting Principle** to change a behavior *directly*. Reconstructing attitudes and expectations relies on the **Recontextualizing Principle** to change a behavior *indirectly*.

"Recontextualizing" expresses the concept of changing the hidden context that frames our realities. We call this hidden context (tacit assumption, paradigm, mindset) an "auto-context" because it is part of our auto-self.

Sometimes the way we view people or situations creates our behaviors. We get angry because we have an *attitude* toward them. This attitude is normally not something that we think about so much as experience emanating from an auto-context that automatically controls our responses.

We can change these reflexive responses by reconstructing an attitude. The first step in reconstructing an auto-context is to make the hidden context explicit. This is a difficult process because we do not normally have easy access to our auto-contexts. We search for the hidden auto-context that creates the attitude through the investigative processes of asking open questions and suggesting possibilities. This give and take between coach/guide and client can take quite a while until the light finally goes on for the client. Even after that, the guide and client may need to continue the investigation to refine the nature of the auto-context that creates the attitude.

Next, we challenge the viability of the context that creates the attitude or expectation and we search for a more functional context that will lead to desired behavioral responses to people or events that used to annoy the client. The client then employs the new context explicitly to enable the desired behavior and practices using the new context explicitly.

Eventually the new explicit context automatically migrates (due to Two-Selfs Property #7: Emergence – auto-self processes imperceptibly emerge to execute repeated activities automatically) into a new auto-context. At that point, normally the new attitude will correct the undesired behavior without any further effort from the client.

Technique: *Probing/Suggesting* to Reveal Hidden Contexts

What This Technique Means:
Sometimes we can change an undesired behavior *indirectly* through **recontextualizing** rather than *directly* through inducing **counteracting** feelings. The first step in this process is to apply probing/suggesting techniques to reveal the contents of the auto-context that drives the dysfunctional behavior.

How to Use This Technique:
Ask questions and make suggestions as coach and client cooperate to reveal a hidden auto-context that creates an attitude or expectation that causes an undesired behavior. The two examples in this chapter demonstrate the use of this technique.

Why This Technique Works:
Sometimes an auto-context, often in the form of an attitude or expectation, underlies an undesirable behavior. If we can make these hidden auto-contexts explicit, we can challenge them and create more-serviceable alternatives. Repeated use of the new explicit attitude or expectation will eventually migrate to a new auto-context that enables the desired behavior.

Revealing and Reconstructing Dysfunctional Attitudes

Mick, the CEO of the auto supply company who we discussed earlier, moved past some of his rages by recontextualizing the hidden assumptions that created his attitude.

We uncovered the auto-context that created his attitude when I asked him why he raged at his employees. With some probing, and after considerable reflection, Mick said it was "because they deserve it."

As we continued to pursue this investigation to make our understanding of the details of his auto-context more specific, he said, "They make a lot of money, so they should not make mistakes."

Mick also complained about the lack of innovation and initiative; everybody came to him for all decisions. He had not yet learned to recognize that he was causing the avoidance behaviors that he disliked so much.

At this point, I recalled a story Mick had previously told me about his skiing experiences, and I decided to use his description of his skiing "zones" as a metaphor to help him understand why the assumptions that underpinned his attitude were not serving him well.

Here is the story Mick previously told me. "I ski in three zones. The green zone is very easy, but I never get any better when I ski there. The red zone is near a cliff, and I am so frightened that I never take any chances, so I also never get any better when I ski there. I have the best fun and I improve the most when I ski in the yellow zone. This zone is difficult for me so I sometimes fall, but it is also safe and I can get up and try again. This making mistakes and getting up and trying again enabled me to ski at the level I do today."

I pointed out to Mick that his anger when his employees made mistakes had taken away the yellow zone in his company. Instead, there was a large complacent green zone and a huge frightening red zone.

Mick's rages created a red zone cliff that caused everyone to retreat to the safe green zone of grudging compliance with little or no risk-taking that independent decision-making and innovation require.

Mick needed to define for others and for himself the boundaries of the red zone where mistakes could have devastating effects on the company.

After that, he needed to open a vast yellow zone where his team could take initiatives and make mistakes without fear of receiving humiliating punishments.

Mick was to point out the mistakes politely so his employees could get back up, brush themselves off, and try to do better next time. That way they would grow and innovate.

Mick got it. His employees did not need punishment when they made a mistake; they needed guidance and encouragement along with boundaries that define the business red zone.

At first, he struggled because he had to remember to apply this new context explicitly, but due to the marvels of the dual human mind, this context eventually migrated to become an auto-context.

Mick no longer rages because his attitude changed, and his company has vastly improved because of it. At the time of this writing, Mick's company was the last remaining Michigan supplier in his niche of the automotive market. Mick led his company to out-execute all of his competition to achieve growth and profitability while still in an economic recession.

Revealing and Reconstructing Dysfunctional Expectations

Gary was a bright, knowledgeable, likable, and well-connected solopreneur (owner of a single-person company). In spite of all of these assets, he was not achieving a level of income he desired and could not break out of this dilemma in order to grow his business. Gary engaged me to coach him with a goal of doubling his income from the previous year. I leveraged my business experience to guide Gary into focusing his offering and repositioning his target market from smaller companies to midsize companies.

My main focus, however, is always on behavior change. We established discipline for Gary by focusing on a hierarchy of quarterly, monthly, and weekly goals. Each week, Gary would set tasks on his calendar to enable him to achieve his weekly goals. I noticed Gary failing to execute his tasks for one particular client. I generally assume that when people do not do what they say they intend to do, hidden discomfort blocks their execution. I focused Gary on the fact that he kept failing to execute for one client and I asked him what was uncomfortable about his work for that client. As normally happens, Gary could not identify any particular discomfort or even notice that discomfort blocked his execution.

I started down a path of proposing possibilities through closed questions. "Is the work very boring for you?" "Do you feel that the work may be too difficult for you?" "Is your client very difficult to work with?" Gary considered each question, and then answered, "No."

I next switched to some open questions and probes. "What does it feel like when work for that client appears on your calendar?" "What do you experience when you work with this client?" "Try to identify what you don't like about working with this client."

After this type of give-and-take over a couple of sessions, we finally zeroed in on what was bothering Gary. Gary was used to having his clients accept the work he delivered to them. This particular client was very bright and challenged Gary's work products. Once we finally discovered the auto-context that was blocking Gary's actions, we were able to work on a recontextualization.

As I kept probing, I discovered that Gary's real fear was that his client would not consider him competent if he did not produce work that was immediately acceptable.

It turned out the client was not abrasive. He just wanted to question Gary's work product to make sure he understood it and to attempt to find improvements.

When I pressed Gary, he admitted his client actually did find some improvements. I then asked Gary what it would be like if he expected this client to help him improve his work product. After struggling a bit, Gary finally realized it would probably create a better result. We finally agreed that Gary would visit his client, tell him how much he appreciated the feedback he gave, and create a working relationship where Gary would bring a draft solution to start the discussions and they would jointly refine the results. After that, Gary readily jumped into his work for this client. He had changed his expectation, so he no longer felt bad when the client worked with him to improve the results.

Many auto-context reconstructions, including self-image changes and business culture realignments, normally produce significant discomfort. Fortunately, most attitude and expectation reconstructions do not create much discomfort. The challenge is to make explicit (i.e., to the thinking-self) the implicit (i.e., buried in an auto-context) assumption that causes an undesired behavior. The persistent use of closed-question suggestions and open-question probing from the transformation guide often uncovers the content of an auto-context that causes the undesired behavior. This is often the easiest path to eliminate an undesired behavior or to overcome a barrier to consistent execution.

18: Posing Evocative Open Questions

Ask a series of evocative questions until the discomfort becomes so great that the client takes the desired action through the path of least discomfort.

Open questions can help people discover and learn for themselves rather than giving them the answer. This form of open questioning goes back millennia to Socrates.

The probing technique of coaching uses open questions as an aid to discover the contents of an auto-context. However, clients rarely discover the content of an auto-context, so we mix probing with suggesting possibilities using closed questions regarding the hidden assumption (auto-context) that may cause the undesired behavior.

We use *evocative* open questions to force clients to realize they are failing to enact their intentions. We ask a series of evocative questions until the discomfort becomes so great that the client takes the desired action through the path of least discomfort.

Here is a summary to the three uses we make of open questions:

- *Socratic open questions* stimulate critical thinking and illuminate ideas.
- The *probing technique* uses *open questions* to help discover the hidden contents of an auto-context.
- *Evocative open questions* evoke feelings to hold people accountable.

You can recognize whether questions are open or closed by the way they begin.

Avoid asking questions that start with "Do you...", "Is it...", "Can you...", "Have you...", or "Does it..." These *closed* questions lend themselves to simple answers and do not create the kind of counteracting feelings we need.

Instead, ask questions that start with something like "Why...", "Please explain...", "How...", or "What..." These *open* questions, which enable the transformation guide to force the client to contemplate a contradictory or inconsistent position, evoke feelings that will counteract the comfort priorities that perpetuate the undesired behavior.

Evocative Questions Get Results for Maria

Maria was a director of software development whom I coached. Maria had strong technical abilities and was a good project manager. However, she was not able to get the best out of her team. One of her intentions for a new behavior was to give balanced performance reviews to her direct reports that noted their strengths but also pinpointed their weaknesses and identified actions to improve their performance. Maria previously had sugarcoated the reviews of her team members. I worked with Maria to develop balanced reviews on her next round. When she kept postponing delivering the reviews, I got her to commit to do two of them before our next coaching session.

At our next coaching session, Maria admitted she had not given the performance reviews. I started with an open question, "Maria, why didn't you conduct those two performance reviews as you intended?"

As expected, Maria replied, "I really wanted to do them, but the week was just so hectic I couldn't hold the schedules."

I could have just told her that this sounded like an excuse and not a reason to me, but I knew she was struggling to give the developmental feedback and I wanted to create some stronger feelings to counteract her discomfort with the performance reviews. I started with what I assumed would be a series of evocative questions as she tried to avoid facing her barrier to action. "What happened to make you so much busier than you thought you would be when you committed to doing the performance reviews?"

Maria rattled off a list of activities that she had not anticipated when she made the commitment.

I continued, "How does that number of interruptions correspond to a typical week?"

Maria answered by repeating the interruptions that kept her from conducting the performance reviews.

I pressed on. "I realize that each week you get interrupted on different issues, but I want you to notice how your interruptions this week corresponded to the amount you should have expected."

Maria was starting to get the point. She finally admitted, "Yes, the amount of interruptions was about normal."

Maria was now running out of wiggle room as I continued to press her. "I assume you plan for your normal amount of interruptions when you schedule important tasks, so tell me again why you didn't do the two performance reviews this week."

This is the crucial point that transformation guides must embrace. Most people find the delay uncomfortable and interrupt the process by asking further questions while the client is still struggling with the previous question. Maria went silent while she tried to think up a way to escape the reality war into which I had led her. I stayed silent and let her grapple with her dilemma.

Maria finally confessed, "Yes, I could have done those interviews. I guess I was just looking for an excuse because I know they will both get upset when I point out their weaknesses."

I now pushed forward to the conclusion of the evocative questions. "Now that you realize what happened last week, what are you going to do differently this week?"

Maria thought a little longer and said she would schedule specific times for the reviews and hold them. This type of evocative question usually gets the desired result. Maria completed the reviews and they went better than she had feared. If I had just suggested that she was offering up excuses, she may have disagreed and not changed her behavior. However, after a series of evocative questions, most people find it preferable to execute their intended behavior than to take another stroll down Evocative Questioning Lane with their coach or guide.

Another powerful use of evocative open questions to change behavior is to apply them while holding somebody accountable who has missed a commitment.

Technique:
Posing Evocative Open Questions

What This Technique Means:
Open questions are ones that people cannot respond with a pat answer such as "yes" or "no."

How to Use This Technique:
If you listen carefully, you will notice that most people ask closed questions most of the time. It takes a lot of practice to learn to ask open questions on the fly. However, it is worth the practice because it is a powerful technique in the transformational coaching/guidance process. The important point is after asking the question to stop and let the client wrestle with trying to resolve the conflict you have created for him or her. The best results usually follow a sequence of questions that force the client to admit failing to execute an intention instead of offering excuses.

Why This Technique Works:
Posing evocative open questions relies on the counteracting principle to change behavior. These questions evoke feelings to counteract the comfort priorities that interfere with success priorities. More specifically, the goal is to keep pursuing the evocative questions until the client eventually executes the intended task due to the *path of least discomfort*.

19: Leveraging Auto-Self Experiences

Once we experience a planned transformation, we can more easily achieve another habit change and better help other people.

It is a bit tricky to learn to observe one of our auto-self's activities and to notice what happens when we transform one of its characteristics. Once a coach/guide helps someone transform, subsequent transformations for that client become easier because the client now has experiential insights into dynamic self-awareness and auto-behavior transformation. The guide can help the client by leveraging the exhilaration of experiencing the old automatic behavior becoming less and less compelling, and the substitute behavior, which starts out feeling unnatural and uncomfortable, becoming easier and more pleasurable to enact.

Rich's New Ability to Drive Results

Rich was the national sales manager for a midsize manufacturing company in the Midwest. He had a technical degree and knew the products and their underlying technologies extremely well. Rich was exceptionally bright and could easily think through complicated scenarios. In spite of his obvious assets, Rich's CEO was considering replacing him because he was not getting needed results out of his sales force. The company decided to try to retain his expertise by hiring my company to coach him to get better results out of his team.

A coach I was training performed the actual coaching, but I attended most sessions as a "shadow coach" to provide feedback to the coach trainee. When we did the performance survey, Rich's shortfalls were obvious. Rich lived in an intellectual world. His keen mind and deep knowledge (i.e., his thinking-self assets) had enabled his previous successes. However, the feedback identified huge gaps in his ability to lead (his auto-self deficiencies). More specifically, he kept telling his team what to do while frequently allowing them to fail to enact his directions. Even his own team identified that he was not leading them effectively.

The first thing we did with Rich was to suggest he transfer to product development or even possibly head up product development for the company. Rich had been a sales executive before in a different environment that enabled some successes for him. He stressed that he was totally committed to succeeding as a sales executive and was prepared to engage fully in the coaching process to overcome his leadership deficiencies.

Rich viewed himself as a nice guy and indeed everything we saw about him concurred with his self-image. We all like nice people, but sometimes in business you have to be tough-minded to get results. Leaders must hold people accountable when they do not achieve results.

We coached Rich to solicit commitments from his team members and then hold them accountable for meeting those commitments. He was to praise them and make them feel great when they achieved their commitments and firmly hold them accountable when they missed them. We role-played with Rich to train him how to ask evocative open questions such as "What does a commitment mean to you?" "What do you think it says to others about your character when you make commitments and fail to keep them?" "Why should we keep you here if you can't do what you promise you will do?" Rich gradually established accountability skills, but he still had a barrier to executing them consistently with his team.

Not surprisingly, Rich gave rosy performance reviews in spite of the fact that most of his team members were missing their numbers. For his next round of performance reviews, we focused Rich on identifying developmental areas in addition to the strengths of his team members. A breakthrough came when Rich decided to rate his top salesperson an "A" on selling the current products but a "D" on selling new products that the company desperately needed to grow revenue. Rich managed to deliver that performance review. This sales person was used to being the star, and now Rich was telling him he was coming up short. This interaction had the desired effect on the sales representative and on Rich. It shook the self-image of the sales person so dramatically that he started focusing on and selling the new products. Rich finally experienced the process and saw the value of applying "tough love" to his salespeople to get them to perform.

As time went on, we kept focusing Rich on learning to hold his people accountable. When, during one of his coaching sessions, we identified a failure in Rich to hold one of his salespeople accountable, Rich retorted that he just could not become a person that slams his fist down and chews people out.

This is the point where we were able to leverage Rich's experience with his star performer. Rich did not shout at him, did not slam his fist down, and did not get aggressive. In order to instill the discomfort needed to create needed actions, Rich calmly told his star that he was coming up short on selling new products. Rich now had an internal experience he could use in other situations. He could ask tough open questions in a calm but firm manner to force his team members to experience the fact that they were not meeting their commitments. Rich went on to leverage his previous experience to become increasingly effective at getting commitments and holding his team accountable. The expected results followed. The company's revenue started growing significantly and the new products took off.

Cecilia's Inability to Lead Effectively

Cecilia was Vice President of Supply Chain Management for a high-tech design and manufacturing company. She had worked her way up the ranks of the corporation to reach the executive level. However, her management had become concerned that while she was a star contract negotiator, she was not getting the best out of her team. The 360° survey and interviews indicated that she lacked the leadership ability to hold members of her team accountable. Like Rich in the previous story, Cecilia lacked the ability to give penetrating developmental performance reviews and to take strong enough actions to get the best out of her team. The fact that Cecilia had worked alongside many of the people she now led compounded her barrier to action.

The breakthrough in Cecilia's coaching came when we identified an auto-self characteristic she had developed in order to succeed in the purchasing world. She could handle the most manipulative and forceful salespeople with a tenacious but calm demeanor in order to get good procurements for her company. What we did was to focus Cecilia on what it felt like when she trained herself to interact effectively in the difficult purchasing environment and what it felt like when she was able to withstand a contentious environment that others would try to escape. This was an "ah ha" experience for Cecilia. She was able to leverage her insights and experiences regarding negotiating good deals out of salespeople in order to "negotiate" better performance out of her team.

Searching for Auto-Self Experiences to Leverage

Most people have experienced one or more auto-self transformations in their lifetimes. Search for them and re-experience them. They can help you transform and can enable you to help others transform. Probably the most common transformation experience is changing from a smoker to a non-smoker. You become a different person in an important way. If you have stopped smoking, you have experienced an auto-self transformation that you can leverage for other transformations. When you stopped smoking, or when you somehow got through another transformation, you most likely did not see it as an explicit automatic-mode transformation. If you re-examine and re-experience that previous change process, it can help you change again in the future and help you guide others through change.

I leveraged my youthful experience of dealing with and finally overcoming road rage. I became convinced we have two selfs and that we can transform aspects of our auto-self; and I leveraged that experience to create the two-selfs theory, to create additional auto-self transformations for myself, and to help many other people through the transformation process.

I always insist that coaches I train go through coaching from the client side so they experience the transformation process they need to create in others.

Leveraging the internal transformation experience is also why peer, or round robin, coaching can help so much. Everyone will experience the process so they can better help their client, and everyone will be able to transform more easily after they learn enough techniques to guide others through a transformation.

Technique:
Leveraging *Auto-Self Experiences*

What This Technique Means:
  "Leveraging Auto-Self Experiences" may seem on the surface to be a restatement of "learn from experience." However, it means more because we now operate within the two-selfs model. "Leveraging auto-self experiences" means explicitly recognizing a successful auto-self characteristic and using it to advantage in another way (as with Cecilia) and recalling the feelings and mechanisms associated with a previous auto-behavior transformation as a means to aid a current transformation.

How to Use This Technique:
  Work with your client to try to identify a previous transformation or a related auto-self ability then draw parallels to the current transformation.

Why This Technique Works:
  Once we experience an internal mental phenomenon, we gain a new insight into what it is and how it works that goes beyond descriptions. A guide can leverage these insights that their clients have to make a new transformation work easier. Guides can also use any direct insights they gain from their habit-change experiences to help transform their clients.

20: Verifying Results

We accomplish what we measure or verify.

Self-help efforts to improve automatic behaviors can lead to success. As such, there is no harm in trying a self-induced transformation.

The harm comes when we allow an attempted self-transformation to become a seduction trap. That is, relieve the internal reality war, created by not changing an unwanted habit, the wrong way by *pretending* we have solved our issue when we have not.

Realistically assessing long-lasting change is one way to stay out of the seduction trap. Ask those around you if you really have stopped your rages. Can you verify that you now hold people accountable when they miss a commitment? Do you routinely eat healthily and exercise regularly? Conscientiously assess if you now regularly take needed actions to accomplish your goals.

Consider retaking a leadership performance survey if you took one before trying the transformation.

If you discover you have not made your desired changes, then you will experience an internal reality war.

The discomfort of realizing that you are failing to achieve your desired change could provide the impetus to restart your self-help effort that had succumbed to the unfair fight in the first place. Alternatively, to improve your chances of success, you could seek help to achieve your desired transformation.

Of course, you should realistically assess results from other auto-self improvement efforts including those conducted by a transformation coach, transformation guide, or an experiential-workshop facilitator.

We need tenacious vigilance and focused techniques to keep the seduction trap from lulling us into a false sense of security.

We accomplish what we measure or verify because knowing the results strips away our ability to pretend we changed when we did not, as happens with many self-help efforts.

Comfort priorities can work for us by helping us accomplish difficult activities or avoid objectionable behaviors, but we have to align them with the needs of our organization or our personal success goals to create sustained success and long-term pleasure.

Remember that short-term comfort often comes at the expense of long-term success.

I measure the effectiveness of my coaching engagements by how much my client, my client's colleagues, and I feel their habits have improved. Sometimes we re-conduct the leadership survey to obtain feedback from colleagues on the actual change. I also typically check in about a year after a coaching engagement ends to make sure there has not been a relapse.

People try to change an auto-behavior when it is important to their success at work or in other aspects of their lives. Whatever method you use to change an undesired auto-behavior, realistically assess the long-term results. If you did not get the results you wanted, you need not give up. Escalate the intervention and try again.

Jake's Results

Jake's biggest challenge was to get through his inability to accept his shortcomings. Everything about Jake's style indicated that once he overcame his resistance to accepting the broad-based feedback, he would do well in coaching. As expected, he approached his coaching experience with the same gusto he approached most everything else in his life.

Halfway into our coaching engagement, it was clear to us all that Jake was going to make the needed changes, so when an opening came up for a regional manager position, Jake got it. Retaining that position was contingent upon him staying with his coaching, but none of us doubted that would happen. Although Jake did not get as relaxed as he would like to at public speaking, he did readily accept opportunities and he acquired sufficient skills to do a credible job. Happily, Jake also reported that at the end of his one-year coaching program, his family unanimously agreed he had made significant changes at home.

Penny's Results

Whereas Jake was all motion with a lot of collateral damage, Penny was mostly lack of execution. Jake had the benefit of a professional transformation coach while Penny had a nonprofessional guide helping her. However, Jeremy was conscientious and patiently guided her for the prescribed year. Penny stepped up easily to learning how to hold her one troublesome employee accountable, and she learned how to get more work out of the two women who reported to her by getting them to give commitments and holding them accountable if they failed to achieve them.

As might be expected, Penny struggled more with her health habits. Her inability to exercise regularly was just another example of her failure at disciplined execution. When she got better at executing at work, she also demonstrated more discipline in her exercise routine (an example of leveraging auto-self experiences discussed in the previous chapter). She established a new exercise habit that will likely stay with her. Her ability to create healthy eating habits was more difficult for her to conquer.

There was more than lack of discipline at work in Penny's inability to control her unhealthy eating habits. Indulgent eating was Penny's go-to escape ritual. Whenever something frustrated her, whenever she got anxious about something, whenever she felt disappointed in herself, she would turn to eating for comfort.

Penny and Jeremy struggled to find a substitute activity to make her feel better when she was having difficult times. They never really found a satisfactory substitute, but the repeated celebration of her steady progress seemed to give her enough good feelings to counteract the drive to eat recklessly. She ended up losing 45 of the 50 pounds she wanted to take off by the time their agreed-to one-year transformation guidance arrangement ended. The good news is that she entered into what appeared to be a wonderful relationship with a man much different from her former husband. Jeremy and Penny were both optimistic that the new relationship would provide both the motivation and the mechanism to help her stay on course with her new healthy habits.

Owning Up to Inevitable Setbacks

Even professional coaches do not achieve 100% success. The disappointments my organization has incurred were obvious early in the coaching engagements and we terminated them quickly.

For all transformation coaches and guides, please remember that the habit change process focuses on enabling clients to change behaviors that they want to change but cannot succeed on their own. Our job is never to impose change. We may need to help our clients to recognize their shortcomings, as previously illustrated successfully with Jake and later shown unsuccessfully with May, but ultimately they need to own the transformation agenda.

A list of our setbacks may help you understand what to look for when guiding someone to change.

May's Inability to Face Shortcomings

May was a bright, technically strong, high-level manager in a large software company. The HR vice president asked me to coach May to help her overcome excessive control needs and relentless micromanaging. May only agreed to enter a coaching program after considerable persuasive efforts on the part of HR and with some restrictions. We conducted a 360° survey and I interviewed several people including current and former direct reports. The feedback was consistent and identified overwhelming behaviors on May's part that were stifling her organization.

I had started coaching May prior to completing the organized performance survey based on the feedback from the HR VP. After May received her leadership performance feedback, she refused to accept it. We tried several approaches over a few weeks as we did with Jake. Jake finally got through the discomfort of discovering his behavioral shortcomings. Unfortunately, May never could do that. The coaching process serves to help people who want to change but cannot transform on their own. Since May was totally convinced she had no issues, there was obviously no point in continuing, so I terminated the engagement. The last time I checked on May's status she had transferred to some limited activity that used her personal talents and avoided her shortcomings. I felt sorry for May because she had enormous talent and could have emerged as a top leader in her company.

Lois Has Trouble with the Truth

Lois was a Ph.D. chief technologist for a high-tech company. She was also a coach's worst nightmare because she was duplicitous – she sometimes had trouble speaking truthfully. The sad thing about some duplicitous people is that they do not even realize they are telling lies. Some people just cannot stand to admit they do not know something or that they have made a mistake, so they make up a story in the hopes that other people will buy it. I think some people do this so often that they start to believe their own fabrications. Sometimes people around them do buy their stories, but over time, many people start to notice their lapses in truthfulness.

I was following my normal process of having Lois log her successes and failures with respect to her intentions for behavior change. I began to suspect that Lois was not reporting accurately about the times when she failed to enact her intended behaviors. It is not a good idea to accuse somebody of telling untruths. I would just express my surprise that she was having so few lapses when I knew how difficult it was for her to make the changes.

As time went on, I started coaching two of her direct reports, who were also friends and supporters of Lois. During my sessions with them, sometimes they would both report activities that were consistent with each other's stories but were inconsistent with reports I was getting from Lois. Now, I no longer just suspected she was not telling the truth, I had solid confirmation.

The next phase of coaching Lois was tricky because I wanted to be as polite as I could and not jeopardize the two people who had reported, quite innocently, different events.

Lois got angry, agitated, and continued to refuse to admit she was not telling the truth and that she was failing to enact her intentions. I knew I could not help Lois change if she could not speak honestly with me when reporting her behaviors, and she did not want to admit and address her duplicity issue, so I terminated the coaching engagement.

Not Fully Engaged

Over the years, we terminated two other coaching engagements early due to lack of desire to change on the part of the client. Stan was head of sales for a venture-backed high-tech company. His management forced him into coaching, and he never wanted to change. He thought his persuasion skills were sufficient to fool us regarding his seriousness to change, but it is quite difficult to fool an experienced coach. His management and I both tried to get him engaged, but to no avail. We terminated the coaching arrangement and his company let Stan go. As they put it, "We really like Stan's sales skills and would like to keep him if he would overcome the issues we identified. We were willing to invest in a coach to help him change. However, when it became clear he didn't intend to change the behaviors that we identified were unacceptable to us, his termination was a no-brainer."

Mack was head of quality assurance for a subsidiary of a high-tech global company in the health industry. He was smart, technically strong, and driven to achieve results. His company engaged me to help him overcome anger and abuse issues. We made some good early progress but then we hit a wall. When he would fail to enact an intention, I would ask him how he felt about it. His usual answer was that he did not feel anything. He thought he did not have any feelings. I tried to help him understand that feelings were driving his behavior, but he could not get it even when he was displaying enormous feelings while stating that he did not have any feelings. We tried engaging another coach who would use a different process from mine, but he hit a similar barrier to a desire to change. Unfortunately, his management ended up terminating Mack because he just did not want to engage fully in the habit-change process.

It is important to persevere with a client even in the face of pushback and disappointments. However, it is also prudent to recognize if the client has given up on the process. The good news for transformation guides is that their clients will normally have a high desire to change, unlike Stan, May, and Mack discussed above.

21: Alan's Case –
Putting It All Together

"I realize I had no chance in the world of ever making the changes without your unwavering help and support." – Alan

Alan's case and the one following illustrate the richness of the transformation techniques described in this book.

Alan, a consultant at a high-end professional services business, had two difficult issues he wanted to transform. His case illustrates the use of most of the techniques described in this book. As such, it goes beyond what we should expect from a transformation guide, but it displays additional examples of habit-change techniques that transformation guides can employ and illustrates the coordinated use of many techniques that professional transformational coaches can employ.

Establishing the Anchors for Change

Alan's company conducted robust performance reviews and had conducted 360° surveys on all of their senior consultants, so when he approached me, he already had a clear static self-awareness. of two troubling issues he wanted to address. He sometimes became visibly angry at work, which was intolerable to his management. He also seemed to have periods where he would perform at a very high level and then would encounter other periods where he struggled to get things done. He did not understand why, but he knew he needed to overcome his down periods in order to continue to prosper in his company.

In Alan's case, his intentions preceded his grand goals. To lock-in the anchors, I invited Alan to declare his intention to curtail his anger outbursts at work and at home and to execute consistently on his projects at work. Alan eagerly declared those intentions.

To make sure Alan did not waver when the going got tough, I also asked him to declare his grand goals for the coaching process. Alan declared that by the end of our one-year coaching engagement he would have reduced any anger displays to an acceptable level at work, as verified in his next performance review, and at home, as measured by feedback from his family. The second grand goal he identified was to receive praise from his boss in his next performance review regarding his consistent performance.

I also made sure that Alan constructed his declarations of intentions and grand goals so that they were unconditional.

Uncontrollable Anger Outbursts

When we started Alan's coaching program, he was eager to eliminate his anger outbursts, which he had repeatedly failed to accomplish on his own. Alan had a solid static self-awareness (he knew he had anger episodes) of his anger control issue, but his dynamic self-awareness (noticing his anger outbursts while displaying them) was spotty. This is common with anger episodes; sometimes people notice while they display them, but other times they erupt without creating solid awareness.

Even as Alan began to read responses from his environment and therefore increase his dynamic self-awareness, he was still not able to control the behavior. As we always do, we had Alan keep a log of any anger outbursts and of the times he felt anger welling up inside him but he maintained his composure. As Alan logged anger "events," he reported a high number of anger outbursts at home. This did not surprise me because behaviors people uncontrollably display at work often appear in other parts of their life. However, Alan was frank about his behavior at home, and he was rightly concerned about the potentially devastating impact he was having on his family. Unfortunately, although his awareness and his honesty in reporting about his anger outbursts at home were laudable, we were not making good progress on curtailing his anger displays.

Alan's Anger at Appliance Store

In a telephone coaching session one week before my next trip to New York for a face-to-face session, Alan presented me with a crucial opening to apply intense virtual conditioning to break his anger outbursts around his family. Alan started out, "Barry, I really messed up two days ago. My wife did some things at a store that I didn't like, and when I got into the car I blasted her in front of our children."

"What did you do in the car, Alan?" I asked.

"I lost control so badly that I can't remember exactly what I said, but it went something like this, 'What do you think you were doing embarrassing me in front of the sales clerk? I had already told him what we wanted to buy when you started asking him a lot of questions about other items.'"

"Whoa, Alan – where were you shopping and what did you want to buy?"

"We were at the local discount appliance store and we were buying a new washer and dryer," Alan replied. "I had done my research and I knew what I wanted to buy. I just needed to negotiate the best possible price. When my wife started asking the sales clerk questions, it just interfered with my negotiations."

"Who does the laundry at your house, Alan?"

"My wife, but that doesn't mean she knows the best washer and dryer to buy."

I was tempted to pursue the line of why Alan did not think his wife should have any input into the decision, but instead I opted for a different approach, asking Alan, "Tell me why you were able to control your anger inside the store but then blew up as soon as you got in the car."

Alan thought for a while and then responded, "I guess I didn't want to make a scene in the store."

Alan had walked into the trap I set for him and I sprung it with a follow-up evocative open question. "Please tell me, Alan, why you find it more important to avoid screaming in front of strangers than in front of your family."

Alan's voice went soft as he responded, "I guess I just didn't want to embarrass myself in front of the salesman and the other people in the store."

I continue my pursuit. I was going to keep pushing the point until his behavior in the car really stung. That is how one instills virtual penalties. "Why is it more important to you to avoid embarrassing yourself with an anger outburst in front of strangers than it is in front of your family?"

There was a long pause while Alan grappled with that question. Even though this was a telephone coaching session, I could tell he was struggling with the reality that he had shown more courtesy to strangers than to his family. Alan finally said meekly, "I don't know why."

I had made my point and I decided to stop that line of questioning for this session. However, it was clear this was a serious problem for his family and I intended to pursue it vigorously when we met face-to-face in a week.

Escalating the Intervention

Several months into Alan's coaching engagement, we had not yet succeeded in curtailing his anger outbursts. I always try to apply the minimum amount of counteracting discomfort to break a bad habit. However, in this case, it was clear he was destroying his marriage, causing damage to his children, and probably harming his career at work, so

I decided to escalate my intervention during our face-to-face session.

I do not want to narrate the details of this difficult session, but I did focus him on the possibility of a divorce and the probability that he was raising his children to be screamers just like him because they would probably mimic his behavior when they had families. I pressed the point so hard that I brought him to tears. This is one of the hardest processes for professional coaches to train themselves to do. It feels terrible to inflict that much discomfort on another person, but my job was to break his anger outbursts and nothing short of a tough session was going to create the transformation. I had to use my coaching techniques on myself to draw counteracting pleasure from the fact that I was coaching him to a point in his life where he desperately wanted to be but could not achieve on his own.

Fortunately, people engaged as a guide to help others should never have to lead such a tough session. If moderate interventions do not work, it is probably better to bring in a professional.

The focus on the impacts to the family was the initiating stimulus to create discomfort. As he was experiencing intense discomfort, I repeatedly focused him on his anger outbursts. This process had the desired effect. Alan's anger outbursts became increasingly uncomfortable. This started to inhibit the auto-self activity that was driving the anger and opened the way for Alan to enact more-appropriate behaviors with increasing frequency. By guiding Alan to celebrate internally every time he succeeded in enacting his new behavior, he gradually became comfortable with his increasingly calmer responses.

Insight: **Three Dimensions of Anger**

When coaching/guiding a client to control anger outbursts, the goal is not complete elimination. Sometimes anger is the appropriate reaction to a serious affront – evolution has constructed our auto-self to react with anger to some situations. Instead, we want the client to gain control over three dimensions of anger responses: **threshold**, **intensity**, and **duration**. The goal is to *increase* the **threshold** (that is, what it takes to create an anger display) to a normal range, *moderate* the **intensity** to avoid collateral damages, and *shorten* the **duration** to get on with normal life.

A Problem with Two-Selfs Theory?

As Alan logged anger events, I noticed an unusual pattern. The vast majority of events Alan reported came from his home life. Our auto-self acts involuntarily, so its actions normally occur in all parts of our lives. Alan's behavior appeared to run counter to part of the two-selfs theory. I expected a proportional number of anger episodes at work.

As expected, Alan did not really understand why he was able to avoid anger outbursts at work better than he was at home. In order to find out why Alan was not having anger outbursts at work as I expected, I employed the probing/suggesting technique.

As I probed into his activities at work, we determined that Alan would escape from situations when he felt his anger rising. He feared he would lose control and create a career-impacting conflict at work. Without fully realizing it, Alan avoided potentially contentious encounters most of the time, but at a high price. He fled when he should have interacted with his colleagues to add value. His fear of losing control resulted in a barrier to certain types of action, which in turn decreased his effectiveness.

As we worked on Alan's anger outbursts at home, which were most of the anger events we had to work with, we also needed to find a way to help him overcome his blockage to engaging in potentially contentious activities at work.

Our two-selfs theory held. Alan wasn't controlling his anger in one venue and not another. Alan avoided situations at work that he felt might cause his anger to overflow.

The Loss of Gusto

In addition to Alan's uncontrollable anger outbursts, which created direct problems for him at home and mostly indirect problems at work, Alan wanted to address a different problem of inconsistent performance.

Alan described this problem as follows. "I have enjoyed many outstanding successes in my career. During those successful endeavors, passion for what I was trying to accomplish always seemed to drive my actions. At other times, I felt I really knew what I needed to do to create another success, but I had to mount a tenacious effort to accomplish all of the needed tasks. However, the worst times of all were when I could not seem to execute all I knew I needed to do to accomplish my goals. I felt so helpless. Moreover, I did not understand why I was not succeeding as I often did, and worse, I was not able do anything about it. My job remained secure for the time because I often did produce outstanding results, but my management made clear to me their dissatisfaction about my periodic failures to execute at a high level."

Alan's barrier to motivated action at certain times almost certainly came from discomfort he felt. I explained to Alan the distinction between success priorities and comfort priorities and suggested that we start searching for his source of discomfort that blocked his peak performance at times.

Alan explained how that felt to him. "I felt a great sense of relief when I learned about the dual, independent priorities that drive our thoughts and behavior. This new distinction enabled me to understand what was driving my puzzling inconsistency in performance. When I was most successful, my comfort priorities aligned with my success priorities. My comfort priorities drove me to accomplish the actions that I knew I needed to execute to succeed. It was as if it did not matter if these actions were required or that others might find some of them difficult to accomplish. I just seemed to do them automatically. The results materialized, and management and colleagues viewed me as a hero because I accomplished so much. I now understand that the pleasure I felt in accomplishing tasks others found very challenging drove me to overcome all barriers to success. I was leading and others were following my lead. I felt unstoppable.

"Unfortunately, sometimes I faltered and my boss even went so far as to accuse me of 'choosing to fail.' I was not 'choosing' to fail. I wanted to succeed. I knew what actions were required, and I did many of them, but I was taking way too long to handle some of them no matter how much I committed to myself to do them. Neither cajoling nor threats from my boss, nor my own determination to succeed, seemed to get me into effective action. My auto-self was blocking my actions in spite of my repeated efforts to execute them."

This was clearly the point where I needed to apply probing/suggesting techniques. I kept asking Alan what specifically it felt like when he could not take a needed action. We do not normally have direct access to the auto-context, often in the form of an attitude or expectation, that blocks an activity. When Alan could not pinpoint what was bothering him, I started suggesting possibilities and watched his responses. "Was the task boring?" "Was it too difficult for you?" "Did it seem like others were taking it in the wrong direction?" This is often a tedious process spanning several coaching sessions.

After a few sessions of probing and suggesting, Alan finally identified what was blocking his actions. Here is how he put it: "A hidden aversion to conflict was keeping me from performing at the necessary level. As we penetrated into the nature of the barriers that were preventing me from executing on some assignments, we found that the issue actually cut two ways. I had an aversion to dealing with aggressive and intimidating people. Apparently, the discomfort was so great that I was avoiding certain people who I needed to interact with to accomplish my assignments. After considerable probing, my coach and I also determined that I had a fear that I would cause conflict when I was interacting with very aggressive people. I unknowingly felt that if I had to deal with aggressive people, I might not be able to control my own temper and might end up embarrassing myself by screaming at them. This also kept me away from certain situations that might lead to potentially contentious interactions."

Exposing Alan's Evasion Gimmicks

Although Alan was eager to engage in the coaching process in order to overcome his undesired behavior patterns, he still occasionally succumbed to using evasion gimmicks. At the beginning of our coaching program, Alan sometimes tried to rationalize that his anger outbursts were really someone else's fault. This was an easy evasion gimmick to overcome. All I had to do was identify it and point him back to his unconditional declarations. He owned his anger outbursts, and he was going to curtail them independent of any person or any situation.

Alan slipped into the use of more evasion gimmicks when trying to overcome his inability to execute consistently. Alan was very smart and loved to do research. Sometimes that was helpful, but when I noticed he was doing it often, I asked him if maybe that was an escape ritual to avoid handling some difficult tasks. After pointing this out a few times, Alan finally agreed. That created sufficient discomfort that Alan eventually did his research only when it was scheduled.

I tracked Alan's progress on all of his projects, and when he fell behind on some, I would ask him why. When his explanation sounded weak to me, I would ask him if he was giving me a reason or an excuse. Sometimes I would accept his explanation as a valid reason. Other times I would ask him about the level of interruptions he expected when he committed to accomplishing certain tasks. Many times, he would recognize that he was not providing a valid reason. Once again, this exposure of an evasion gimmick forced him to face that he was failing to enact his intention, which normally caused him to get back into action through the path of least discomfort.

Leveraging Progress on Anger Management

Once Alan finally began to transform his anger at home, we were able to leverage that experience to help him with other transformations. Alan now had direct insight into what it was like to observe his auto-self's activities and to experience a transformation.

At work, Alan started noticing when he disengaged from activities that he needed to engage in. He also became confident that he would notice when his anger started to rise and that he would be able to substitute an appropriate behavior before he created any external displays of his rage. He was able to leverage his insights from his previous transformation to change the way he interacted at work.

As Alan became increasingly adept at constructing dynamic self-awareness of a particular auto-self activity, he started noticing when he failed to take needed action and pinpointing the nature of the feeling that was blocking him. Often, it was a fear of losing control of his emotions that preempted his active engagement. Over time, Alan was able to recognize this barrier and some other barriers that were blocking his passionate engagement. Alan's previous transformation created confidence he could make another one, which led him to regain his gusto in most situations.

Recontextualize – Attitude Change

In addition to heavy doses of virtual consequences, I also helped Alan reconstruct some attitudes. I came back to that episode in the appliance store several times. When I probed about his concept of a family, he finally was able to unpack his attitude towards his family. He believed he was "king of the realm" or "lord of the manor." When we finally made that auto-context explicit, Alan realized that was not the way to treat his wife or work with her to raise their children. Just because he was a big deal at work did not make him the boss at home. He proceeded to create an explicit attitude regarding his role in the family. As usual, after using that explicit context for a while, it eventually migrated to an auto-context (Two-Selfs Property #7: Emergence – Auto-self processes imperceptibly emerge to execute repeated activities automatically).

Successful Conclusion

Alan transformed his anger outbursts because he was able to manage all three dimensions of anger damage. Alan no longer had a hair-trigger for his anger outbursts. He had raised the threshold that triggered his anger response to a normal level. The virtual penalties that I instilled in him created such discomfort when he noticed an anger outburst that he greatly lowered the intensity and stopped very quickly whenever he did become angry.

This coaching engagement went beyond what we should expect a friend or colleague to accomplish when guiding someone through transformational change. However, it illustrates many of the techniques discussed in this book and shows how guides can use them in less intense situations. Alan's transformation required a combination of intense virtual conditioning, recontextualizing, stripping away evasion gimmicks, and leveraging the first difficult transformation to enable subsequent changes.

While this engagement lasted a bit longer than we usually target, Alan successfully reduced his anger outbursts to occurring only in extreme situations. As we would expect, his situation improved both at work and at home. We provided this example to illustrate that the intensity of the virtual penalties and virtual rewards must match the tenacity of the auto-self resistance to change. In this rather extreme situation, Alan's discomfort escalated towards pain. In the previous examples, much less intense emotions were involved.

As we concluded our coaching program, Alan thanked me for all I had done for him. He even told me that his wife sent her thanks for all the changes he had made. He also noted the support I gave him throughout the process. Here is how he expressed it, "Barry, you were very tough on me during many of our coaching sessions, but I realize it requires inducing a lot of feelings to change deep-seated habits. I also appreciate that in spite of all of your tenacious pushing of me, you also repeatedly focused me on my goals and kept encouraging me to achieve them. I realize I had no chance in the world of ever making the changes without your unwavering help and support."

I usually follow-up about one year after I stop a coaching engagement to check on the status of my clients' transformations. In Alan's case, I did not need to follow up. He called me before the year was out to thank me again and tell me the transformations he made had indeed stuck and that his company had just promoted him to a management position. He also shared that his family life had improved considerably.

22: Brad's Case –
Exceeding Expectations

"The greater danger for most of us is not that our aim is too high and we miss it, but that it is too low and we reach it." – Michelangelo

Anemic Expectations

Brad, the manager of human resources for a Midwestern manufacturing company, approached me to coach his CEO who had a bad temper and intimidated people. Paul, the CEO, then commissioned a leadership survey of the top managers in the company. Besides conducting an online 360° leadership survey, my organization interviewed several people. I interviewed Brad. When I asked him where he would like to be in five years, he answered, "Employed." That obviously was not a very empowering outlook. At the time, Brad reported to an executive who reported to the CEO.

While I was coaching Paul through his intimidating behavior, I also conducted some informal coaching for Brad. When I found out that Paul deliberately avoided conducting performance reviews because he did not think they helped, I persuaded him of the value and I coached him through the process of setting up meetings and conducting performance reviews for all for his direct reports, with Brad's help to prepare for each review. When we finished the process, I asked Brad to take over helping

Paul for the future. Brad responded, "I can't do that – I can't tell Paul what to do."

I pointed out to Brad that as head of HR, he should take the responsibility for doing it and if I could work the process from the outside, he could work it even better from the inside. Even though Paul had moderated his behaviors, Brad was still terrified of him.

As time went on and Brad became increasingly comfortable with the new Paul, he became more effective to the point where Paul promoted him to Director of HR reporting directly to him.

After coaching Paul through his aggression episodes and a few other issues, getting him focused on developmental performance reviews, and guiding him to ask open questions in meetings to develop his team members, we had many aspects of the company running well. Paul was strong in technology, in manufacturing, and in finance – he knew how to create profitable businesses. He also was a ferocious problem solver.

Oblivious to Greater Possibilities

What Paul lacked was the patience to focus on the day-to-day execution of the many projects and tasks required to sustain success. Since Paul disclosed having a form of attention deficit disorder, it did not seem productive to coach him to lead the charge on methodical execution. Instead, we wanted to complement Paul with somebody who could assure the execution of the directions that Paul so ably set. One possibility would have been to go outside and hire a COO (Chief Operating Officer) — an expensive path that also would mean bringing in somebody who did not know the business well. We felt that none of the plant managers had what it took to assume that corporate role.

Brad had been making good progress in his ability to interact with Paul and had been taking an increasing role in driving results. As Paul and I discussed how to complement his abilities with a more methodical executive, we concluded that Brad might fill that role if I coached him to operate at a more senior level.

Brad had become solid as head of HR, but he could not envision himself in a much greater role. He needed more confidence and additional techniques. Brad wanted Paul to tell him what to do, but Brad needed to figure out what to do on his own to assume the senior operating role.

Paul and I saw possibilities in Brad that Brad could not see himself. Brad initially resisted getting involved in coaching. Since he did not have significant aspirations or empowering self-confidence, he was unable to visualize a greater future for himself. Paul acted correctly by not insisting that Brad enter a coaching program. However, Paul and I continued to offer coaching to Brad as a possibility. Eventually, Brad decided to receive coaching.

Reaching the Next Level through Coaching

When I interviewed people around Brad at work as a normal prelude to a coaching engagement, I found auto-self issues that Brad would do well to improve. He often failed to pay close attention during meetings, so he sometimes would ask a question about something previously discussed. He would frequently talk over people when they were speaking to him. He was viewed as being overly pessimistic – a glass-half-empty kind of guy. These issues were the starting point for his coaching program, but Paul and I had much greater expectations than correcting Brad's minor deficiencies. We intended to develop Brad to take on significantly greater responsibilities.

After the departure of the CFO, Brad assumed responsibility for driving the strategic planning process. He did a good job of getting all the key players together and leading the way to identify some viable strategic directions. However, during the next year he was not able to drive the execution of the strategic plan into the operating plans. He lacked the ability to hold people that did not report to him accountable.

Since lack of accountability ran rampant in their company, Paul and Brad asked me to conduct a commitments/accountability workshop series. As part of Brad's development, I asked him to co-facilitate the workshop on commitments/accountability. That helped establish Brad as a top leader in the company and it provided an excellent opportunity for him to learn to hold his colleagues accountable and lead the process of improving the accountability culture in the company.

As I coached Brad to operate at a higher level, he pleaded that he was too busy and just could not take on much more. I then challenged Brad to offload 50% of what he was currently doing so that he could take on higher-level activities. At that point, he could not imagine how we could offload that much activity and he could not visualize how he could usefully fill up so much additional time.

Fortunately, Brad had a capable assistant at one of the plants, Lucy, who appeared to have more potential if we could get her to offload some of what she was doing. The plan was falling into place. Brad was to offload 50% of what he currently did to Lucy and then hire a plant HR person to whom Lucy could offload some of her work. Lucy already handled some corporate work for Brad; now she would take on more.

I also coached Brad to take more responsibility for holding colleagues accountable. Gradually, he stepped up to this increased responsibility.

Brad still sometimes waits for Paul to tell him what to do or to give him permission to take needed actions, but he has come a long way. Brad is learning to lead at a higher level. He is becoming a star performer at a level almost unimaginable before he experienced coaching.

Training to Coach

As Brad started freeing up time, we had the opportunity to introduce him to new activities. As a further part of Brad's development, and as a means to develop others and provide in-house coaching expertise, I began training Brad as a coach. I "shadow coached" (monitored Brad's coaching sessions and occasionally coached – usually when Brad invited me in at the end of each issue) Brad as he coached three different leaders with vastly different needs and personalities and therefore needing three different coaching approaches. Brad made excellent progress on all but the most difficult aspects of coaching.

The areas where Brad struggled provide insights into where transformational guides and inexperienced coaches may fall short. Brad had difficulty constructing open questions, as most untrained people do. After most sessions, Brad and I would debrief on how he did at coaching. I would usually point out that he asked too many closed questions that were not stimulating thinking or evoking feelings. After a while, Brad would notice his closed questions after he asked them and restate them as open questions after getting a terse response. As time went by, Brad got increasingly better at constructing evocative open questions on the fly.

After Brad learned to construct powerful open questions, he had another barrier he needed to overcome. He would get uncomfortable and ask another question instead of waiting for his coaching clients to struggle through formulating acceptable answers. This issue was related to his habit of talking over people when in normal conversations. Brad started coaching others while I was still coaching him, so we were able to work simultaneously on his over-talking issue and his struggle to wait for answers. He needed to listen better. Happily, Brad has not only learned to construct potent open questions, he now also pauses while his clients struggle with their answers.

As Brad has continued coaching others, he has become increasingly competent – demonstrating a keen ability to search for evasions, ask timely pointed questions, and keep his clients/colleagues on a path to enact their intentions and achieve their grand goals.

As an example, without prompting from me, Brad challenged his clients to develop their team members better so they could offload more to them. He explained that this was the way for them to assume higher-level responsibilities. This move by Brad provides yet another example of how experiencing an internal auto-self shift makes it easier to coach other people through it.

Brad's major remaining challenge is to induce virtual rewards and virtual penalties at the level dictated by the situation.

We were failing to make adequate progress in coaching Larry, one of Brad's internal clients. I suggested to Brad that he needed to induce some virtual penalties to get Larry over a major hurdle that was blocking his success. Brad pushed back. He said, "You don't understand, Barry. If I make Larry very uncomfortable, it might hurt my relationships with him and I have to keep working with Larry after this coaching program is over." To me, that was Brad's excuse for avoiding the discomfort of inducing virtual penalties.

I have seen such reluctance before with people I have trained to coach. For most of us, it takes considerable conditioning to accept this discomfort. However, getting people occasionally annoyed with us during the coaching process is the norm. After all, we are pushing them to do something that they have declared that they want to do but that they find uncomfortable and still try to avoid. After having been through this process many times, I have found that clients seem to forget about the difficult moments and rejoice in the successful transformation once it occurs. They realize that without the persistent nudging they would never have achieved the changes they desired.

Since I was no longer formally coaching Brad, we did not have sufficient opportunity to get him through this barrier so we decided that I would come to town to apply virtual conditioning face-to-face with Larry. That session had the desired effect. I moved Larry past a major barrier that was keeping him from executing some crucial activities effectively.

Brad learned from this experience. Here is how he put it. "I like the way you handled this, Barry. You did not get aggressive with him and you did not insult him. You just kept pressing open questions that made him squirm and reflect upon his lack of progress." During this session, Brad and I reversed roles; I took the lead and he occasionally coached, and Brad landed one potent open question. After the session when Brad and I debriefed, I congratulated him on posing a timely open question and asked if he noticed that he failed to look at Larry when he asked the question. To Brad's credit, he did notice and commented that it was just too uncomfortable for him to look straight at Larry while asking the question. Brad also said he noticed that I made eye contact throughout my interactions with Larry.

Brad still needs to overcome his final major hurdle because he will need the same skills and the same ability to withstand the discomfort of pushing people through their resistance to change as he assumes increasing responsibility to drive consistent results in the company.

Exceeding His Own Expectations

What a joy it is to help a leader in his late fifties exceed his own wildest dreams of success and accomplishment. And people claim you can't teach an old dog new tricks.

Brad resisted entering into coaching. Also, periodically during his coaching, he suggested not continuing. He kept focusing on addressing his shortcomings, and when he corrected them, he wanted to stop the coaching process. However, his undesired behaviors were not overwhelming, and Paul and I wanted to focus on developing new capabilities. Brad could not see greater possibilities. Such is the nature of our auto-self that he could not visualize his potential. Fortunately, Paul and I did see his potential and moved Brad along, even if somewhat reluctantly on his part, to realize that potential.

At the time of this writing, Brad continues to assume greater responsibilities. He is well on his way to taking over responsibility for overall execution – essentially the COO role.

Brad's case provides an excellent example of people exceeding their own expectations and of how they can learn through coaching to execute and lead at successive levels above their own wildest imaginings.

The plan worked out extremely well. Instead of hiring a COO, Brad took over the top operating role while still maintaining overall guidance of HR and direct responsibility for people development. Brad promoted Lucy to the position of manager corporate HR. By developing Brad to operate at a higher level and then having him challenge and develop Lucy to assume responsibilities for half of what he used to do, the one new hire was a plant HR generalist instead of a more expensive COO. Even with well-deserved raises for Brad and Lucy due to their promotions and greatly increased responsibilities, the company saved significant money and dramatically improved overall performance by systematically developing and getting the best out of the talent they already had.

23: The Next Frontier
for Maximizing Performance

Transformable leaders and organizations will become the main sources of sustainable competitive advantage.

Ignorance Is Not Bliss

A colleague, Gloria, once complained to me, "Many people have told me how smart I am. I had many early successes. I just assumed that being smart, getting a good education, and working hard were all it took to succeed. Then I noticed that some people who didn't seem very bright were moving ahead of me. What happened?"

What happened was that Gloria only developed part of what it takes to succeed. She suffered from stunted potential because she did not understand the existence of her auto-self and how to improve it systematically. No one ever guided her to lead effectively, to avoid displaying annoying behaviors, or to execute consistently on topics she did not enjoy.

Enabler or Saboteur?

Are you fooling yourself? The candid answer is that sometimes we all engage in self-deception.

Do you notice when your auto-self is your *enabler* or your *saboteur*? Since your auto-self if always active, most of the time it is one or the other, and you would do well to find out which it is in your pursuits of success in your profession and in your life in general. You had better make it your enabler most of the time.

We need to ascend from fooling ourselves to conquering our two selfs.

The Two-Dimensional Territory

Understanding the existence of our dual mind and learning to manage the automatic mode is not a small step. Two-selfs theory and techniques create the *next frontier* in performance improvement toward authentic and sustainable success. It is now possible to traverse the boundaries of this two-selfs frontier and enjoy the benefits available in the new performance-maximizing territory.

We experience the territory behind the performance-improvement frontier as exhilarating and powerful because a two-dimensional human mental world suddenly opens up for us. In this new two-dimensional world, we can now conquer the auto-self. Once we occupy this new terrain, we can systematically improve execution and ameliorate disruptive behaviors that cause so much collateral damage.

Winning is fun, but the path to winning is often uncomfortable and even scary because it requires <u>delaying gratification</u> and <u>counteracting the discomfort</u> associated with *transformational change*.

This book has presented theory and techniques to allow non-experts to guide others to transform undesired behaviors using techniques built upon the Counteracting Principle, which induces feelings to counteract the auto-self feelings that drive undesirable habitual behaviors and create the inherent resistance to transformational change.

Don't let the number of techniques you have seen in this book intimidate you. You can guide a direct report, a colleague, or friend through transforming undesired behaviors or debilitating barriers to success even if you use only the following techniques:

- Guide clients to *declare* **anchors** (grand goals and intentions).
- Provide repeated **support** in the form of encouragement and a vision of achieving grand goals.
- Assure that your clients regularly **log** successes and failures for intentions.
- Create **dynamic self-awareness** of the unwanted behaviors – clients must notice them.
- Expose **evasion gimmicks** to keep clients from avoiding needed actions.

Even if you never become competent at instilling virtual consequences or using the other complicated techniques described in this book, the above techniques will make a great difference over self-transformation for someone you want to improve through transformation guidance.

To maximize successes at transformational change, plan to provide guidance twice per week, normally on the phone, even for just a few minutes if just one auto-behavior is involved.

Don't appeal to logic (a thinking-self activity). To create auto-behavior change, you must induce feelings (an auto-self activity):

- Induce pleasure (in forms such as accomplishment, pride, success, and walking the talk) when clients enact their intentions.
- Induce discomfort (in forms such as frustration, disappointment, embarrassment, and not walking the talk) when clients fail to enact their intentions.

Transformation Guides and Coaches

How do transformation guides differ from professional transformation coaches? Having trained transformation coaches, I have good insight into what new coaches struggle to master in the intricacies of guiding people to transform undesired behaviors.

Expert coaches have:

- conditioned themselves to withstand the personal discomfort from their clients. pushback and from deliberately inducing discomfort in their clients
- practiced to recognize a wide variety of evasion gimmicks and techniques to expose them
- mastered a rich repertoire of counteracting techniques including virtual conditioning
- conquered the difficult process of constructing evocative open questions and withstanding the discomfort of pausing while their client struggles to construct a viable answer

Transforming auto-behaviors can help you transform people who report to you. In addition, the concepts and techniques you have encountered in this book will work the other way around. You can recruit a colleague or friend to guide you to improve your successes in all aspects of your life. Transformation coaching/guidance can enable you to maximize your productive behaviors and to minimize or eliminate any disruptive behaviors. It allows transcending your involuntary, robot-like limitations and excesses.

Transformable Leaders

Reaching our potential is a moving target as we traverse successive transformations. We can reconstruct only limited aspects of who we are during any one transformational improvement cycle. However, as we re-stabilize after each transformation and consolidate our newly developed abilities, we open up new possibilities for still greater improvements.

People who are prepared to devote and accept the time, energy, commitment, and occasional discomfort to enact periodic transformations can experience a series of extraordinary improvements toward greater achievement and sustainable success. It is realistically possible to reach successive levels of accomplishment that exceed anything you can currently contemplate. You should aspire to become a **transformable leader** and create other transformable leaders in your organization.

If you want to *lead* better, coach. If you want to *be* better, receive coaching.

Principle: **Transformable Leaders**

Transformable leaders are those who periodically seek out and accept feedback on their auto-self characteristics and engage in activities to transform their comfort priorities to align with success needs. These transformable leaders, who periodically undergo transformations and who help others transform, will be the star leaders of the future.

Transformable leaders become resilient. They recover from any bad breaks and avoid setbacks by periodically transforming to perform at successively higher levels. They also avoid blindsided derailment by periodically receiving feedback and getting help to leverage their auto-self strengths and to overcome their auto-self limitations.

Transformable Organizations

Just as **transformable people** will be the star leaders of the future, **transformable organizations** will achieve a sustainable competitive advantage for a long time – until their competitors "train in" techniques for improving the auto-self to maximize performance.

Principle: **Transformable Organizations**

In today's global economy, all organizations have ready access to technology, natural resources, capital, and smart, knowledgeable people. The best source of sustainable competitive advantage in the future will accrue to those organizations that become transformable; that is, to organizations that periodically assess the auto-self characteristics of their leaders and systematically provide support in the form of experiential workshops, peer transformation guidance, and professional coaching to align the automatic activities of their leaders with evolving organizational needs.

If you lead people, you have a responsibility to improve their performance. If any of your direct reports have persistent barriers to crucial actions or display undesired behaviors, you cannot change these ineffective habits by just talking to them. You need to coach them to change their counterproductive auto-behaviors – you must become a transformation guide for people who report to you. Use this book as your performance-improvement manual so you can attain star performance out of your team members.

You can use this transformation manual to help others or to have someone else help you. It provides the process to transform to a better, more powerful, more in-control tomorrow.

Transformable *leaders* **and** *organizations* **will become the main sources of sustainable competitive advantage.** Using this book as a transformation manual can help you achieve both goals.

**Create Stars and Become a Star
through Conquering the Auto-Self**

Epilogue

My goal is that you achieve more successes than you ever thought possible at work, in your life, and in helping others.

I have spent two decades developing the concepts and improvement techniques in this book both as an executive with thousands reporting to me, and as a transformational coach helping leaders overcome their limitations and establish new abilities.

I, and coaches I trained, have demonstrated repeatedly that these habit-change techniques work effectively. I hope that you have found them accessible and useful and that they have already begun to help you transcend your involuntary limitations and excesses, leverage your hidden strengths, and help others make improvements beyond their own expectations.

Please contact me if you would like help in deploying these transformation strategies and techniques within your organization.

Penetrating our two selves opens up a new frontier. I will explore and describe more of the territory behind that frontier in future writings.

The Next Book about Our Auto-Self

The next book in this series will cover **auto-contexts**, which play a pivotal role in individual and organizational success. Auto-contexts provide the "lenses" through which we interpret the world around us. They are hidden assumptions (often referred to as paradigms, mindsets, mental models, cultures, the "box") buried in our auto-self. Auto-contexts both enable and constrain our thought patterns and what appears as real to us. They create a framework that plays a crucial role for communication and cooperative activities within a stable environment. However, inherent resistance to auto-context change, similar to auto-behavior resistance to habit change, creates debilitating barriers to success when the individual or organizational environment changes to a point where the existing auto-contexts (hidden, often implicit assumptions) become dysfunctional.

Additional Books to Leverage the Auto-Self

Subsequent books will build upon the first two by applying insights and transformation techniques for auto-behaviors and auto-contexts (along with auto-skills and auto-expertise) to specific industries or domains. Areas ripe to benefit from auto-self concepts and change techniques, and that I intend to address in future books, include business, education, and prisoner rehabilitation.

In **business**, dual-mind accessibility opens up an explicit way to handle issues that leaders loosely describe and haphazardly manage now as "soft success factors." Understanding the auto-self also creates a new and more powerful way to understand and manage leadership and leadership development because the auto-self controls most leadership activities. In addition, the ability to create transformable leaders and organizations will establish a significant competitive advantage for companies and other organizations that "train in" this ability.

In **education**, we currently miss a huge opportunity for developing abilities in future generations by failing to teach about our two selfs and how to manage our automatic mode for greater career and life successes. Historically, societies that learned to teach science and technology enjoyed a long-term competitive advantage over societies that remained stuck in pre-science learning programs. Many formerly underperforming societies have now upgraded their education systems to teach science and technology and are emerging as major competitors on the world stage using market economies. Most educational programs have become good at instilling knowledge to maximize the effectiveness of our thinking-self. The next wave of competitive advantage for whole societies will belong to those that teach their students about the dual nature of our mind, the existence and nature of our automatic mode, and how to improve the auto-self systematically. Previous competitive advantage for whole societies due to widespread scientific and technological abilities emanated from "teaching in" these abilities for teachers. Likewise, future competitive advantage for whole societies due to widespread conquering of the auto-self will emanate from "training in" these abilities for teachers. We need our education systems to migrate from about 1.1-dimensional to 2-dimensional so students can conquer the auto-self.

For **prisoner rehabilitation**, the two-selfs theory offers new hope for overcoming the problem of increasingly unmanageable incarcerations and discouragingly high rates of recurring infractions of the law by ex-prisoners that return them to prison. Prison systems provide prolonged periods of densely populated confinement, but they do little to help prisoners "go straight," and the rate of repeat offenses demonstrates that current approaches are not working. What little effort most prison systems make toward rehabilitation consists of attempts to teach directly, which only involves the thinking-self and is, therefore, of limited effectiveness. Prisoners need transformations of their dysfunctional auto-behaviors (habits) and auto-contexts (attitudes and expectations). A program of one-on-one transformational coaching would likely create dramatic results, but, given that there are millions behind bars, the investment is too high for pragmatic implementation. Instead, I visualize, and intend to develop, a program of facilitated reciprocal transformation guidance that could lower recidivism systematically and save societies huge expenses and social problems.

Feedback from You

Please share your successes and suggestions with me, as my greatest joy comes from knowing how I have enabled others build better lives. Who knows? You may even end up in one of my future books as a case study, and your suggestions and insights might help others improve.

I wish you all the successes you deserve!

Barry Borgerson

Barry@2Selfs.com

Appendix A: Auto-Self Principles

Overarching/Foundational Principle   **Humans Have Two "Selfs"**

Principles of the Two-Selfs Theory

Auto-Self Affects Success 4 Ways

Dual Priorities

Evasion Gimmicks

Unfair Fight

Transforming for Success

Self-Transformation is an Unfair Fight

Repeated Support

The **Counteracting** Principle

Static Self-Awareness

The **Recontextualizing** Principle

Dynamic Self-Awareness

Two-Selfs *Properties*

Behavior-Change Anchors

Virtual Conditioning

Realigning Comfort Priorities

Reconstructing Attitudes and Expectations

Transformable Leaders

Transformable Organizations

Appendix B: Two-Selfs Properties

Two-Selfs Property #1: **Control**

Automatic, involuntary, robot-like

Intentional, voluntary, thought/story-based

Two-Selfs Property #2: **Awareness**

Operates outside normal awareness

Center of awareness; consumes awareness

Two-Selfs Property #3: **Simultaneity**

Many processes execute simultaneously

Single task (thought, story) at a time

Two-Selfs Property #4: **Detection of Events**

Can detect many external and internal events

Misses most external and internal events

Two-Selfs Property #5: **Redirected Thoughts**

Can redirect thought stream ("daydreaming")

Gets redirected by auto-self (often unnoticed)

Two-Selfs Property #6: **Progression of Detection**

Can detect internal events progressively earlier

Does not progress when it notices an event

Two-Selfs Property #7: **Emergence**

Processes imperceptibly emerge to execute repeated activities automatically

Requires focused attention and effort

Two-Selfs Property #8: **Induced Feelings**

Can induce feelings from external/internal cues

Normally operates free of strong feelings

Appendix C: Transformation Techniques

Auto-Behavior Transformation Techniques

Providing Repeated Support

Constructing a Path of Least Discomfort

Establishing *Dynamic* Self-Awareness

Logging Execution of Intentions

Declaring Behavior-Change Anchors

Instilling Virtual Consequences

Exposing Evasion Gimmicks

Probing/Suggesting to Reveal Hidden Contexts

Posing Evocative Open Questions

Leveraging Auto-Self Experiences

Index:

105
auto-skills, 44, 61, 141,
306
Barbara [case study], 204,
214
barriers to action, 106
behaving non-
disruptively, 51
Behavior Change: A View
from the Inside Out
[book], 13
behavior-change anchors,
declaring, 172
best-practices books, 18
Bossidy, Larry, 12, 70
brain vs. mind, 18
Bruce [case study], 68,
85, 119, 120
Butler-Bowdon, Tom, 114
Carnegie, Dale, 224
CDO (chief
demotivational officer),
51
Cecilia [case study], 254
Center for Creative
Leadership, 153, 154
characteristics, auto-
behavior, 57, 156
characteristics, auto-self,
57, 71, 93, 156, 157,
191, 193, 300
Charan, Ram, 12, 70
Chayes, Michael, 154
coach, advisory, 132
coach, master, 117
coach, training, 289
coach, transformation,

133
comfort priorities, 63, 65,
72
comfort priorities,
realigning, 220
competing priorities, 67
conditioning, operant,
219, 226
conditioning, parents, 33
conditioning, patriotism,
33
conditioning, virtual, 217,
218, 271
conscious competence,
213
conscious incompetence,
213
consequences,
environmental, 222
consequences, future, 226
consequences, real, 226
consequences, virtual,
222, 226
contexts, hidden, 239
counteract, 73, 129, 143
counteract habit-change
discomfort, 170
counteracting feelings,
139
counteracting feelings,
induce, 150
Counteracting Principle,
137, 138, 159, 237
counteraction techniques,
143, 148
Cyril [Jake's coach], 25,
160, 181

www.ingramcontent.com/pod-product-compliance
Lightning Source LLC
Chambersburg PA
CBHW060323200326
41519CB00011BA/1820